"I wish I had *Get Closer* years ago when beginning my first partnership. Jeffrey Chernin is wise, has tons of common sense and street smarts and knows when adaptability and, contrariwise, holding fast are needed in relationships. A terrific and useful book."

—Felice Picano, coauthor of *The New Joy of Gay Sex*

"Jeffrey Chernin has done a great job helping gay men get closer! He guides us through our readiness for a relationship and how to find a likely partner. Then he provides helpful strategies to work through the differences that inevitably arise, enhancing our ability to maintain the intimate connections many of us long for."

—Rik Isensee, LCSW, author of *Love Between Men*

"*Get Closer* is an outstanding book for gay men who want to look at their relationships—both beginning and long-term—and improve them. Improving our relationships means that we have to learn how to get closer to our partner—to become intimate. This book will help you to get closer to yourself and to others!"

—Kenneth D. George, Ph.D., Emeritus Professor,
University of Pennsylvania, author of
Mr. Right Is Out There and *Keeping Mr. Right*

"*Get Closer* is a persuasive and accessible guide to achieving intimacy. Effective and succinct, it illustrates how genuine intimacy can truly minimize legal conflicts in our most important relationships."

—Frederick Hertz, attorney/mediator,
coauthor of Nolo Press's *Legal Guide for Lesbian & Gay Couples*

GET CLOSER

A GAY MEN'S GUIDE TO INTIMACY AND RELATIONSHIPS

Jeffrey N. Chernin, Ph.D., MFT

alyson books
NEW YORK

© 2006 BY JEFFREY N. CHERNIN. ALL RIGHTS RESERVED.

MANUFACTURED IN THE UNITED STATES OF AMERICA.

THIS TRADE PAPERBACK ORIGINAL IS PUBLISHED BY ALYSON BOOKS,
P.O. BOX 1253, OLD CHELSEA STATION, NEW YORK, NEW YORK 10113-1251.
DISTRIBUTION IN THE UNITED KINGDOM BY TURNAROUND PUBLISHER SERVICES LTD.,
UNIT 3, OLYMPIA TRADING ESTATE, COBURG ROAD, WOOD GREEN,
LONDON N22 6TZ ENGLAND.

FIRST EDITION: JUNE 2006

06   07   08   09   00   **a**   10   9   8   7   6   5   4   3   2   1

ISBN 1-55583-865-0
ISBN-13 978-1-55583-865-2

LIBRARY OF CONGRESS CATALOGING-IN-PUBLICATION DATA IS ON FILE.

COVER PHOTOGRAPH BY STOCKBYTE.

AUTHOR PHOTOGRAPH BY ALEX YOUSEFI.

CONTENTS

Acknowledgments vii

Introduction ix

Chapter 1: Gay Men and Intimacy 1

Chapter 2: Getting Ready for a Relationship 11

Chapter 3: Meeting and Dating Men 27

Chapter 4: Early Intimacy. 42

Chapter 5: What to Expect as You Get Closer 57

Chapter 6: Building the Foundation for Deeper Intimacy . .84

Chapter 7: Understanding Relationship Dynamics . . 100

Chapter 8: Changing Relationship Dynamics 118

Chapter 9: Negotiating Gay Relationships
in a Straight World 131

Chapter 10: Challenges Over Time 150

Chapter 11: The Biggest Threats 166

Chapter 12: Communication Tools for Restoring
and Enhancing Intimacy 183

Chapter 13: Achieving Genuine Intimacy 197

Resources 213

Index 216

ACKNOWLEDGMENTS

To my wonderful parents, Anne and Mickey, and to my sisters Sheila and Mallorie, and Mallorie's husband, John, and my nieces and nephew. And to all my friends. Special thanks to Herb Tums, Dewey Nichols, Jay Newberry, Dave Collier, and Oren Raz. Many thanks for your encouragement and feedback.

Thank you to all my colleagues at 6310, especially Dr. Faith Szalay, Ross Harpold, Mark Danson, Jan Reynolds, and interns Heather and Donna. To my former supervisors turned colleagues, Carolyn Solis and Dr. Melissa Johnson, who planted the seeds by presenting intimacy workshops at Oak Lawn Community Center in the early 1990s. To my professors and mentors, especially Jan Holden, Robert Berg, Cindy Chandler, and Doug Norton. To my former staff at Campion Mental Health Center: Pam, Maggie, Susan, Sherly, Allison, Catita, Michael, Linda, and Sarah: you were the best staff anyone could ever ask for and I miss you all!

To Nick Street, for getting a green light for the project. And to Shannon Berning at Alyson, who has been instrumental in shaping the book and offering valuable feedback.

To the person who has been caring, patient, and supportive through the process of writing this book and throughout our relationship: This book is lovingly dedicated to Peter Nardi, a kind and generous man who is magically smart with a maddening memory, not to mention a great sense of humor. Thank you, thank you, thank you for being you and for becoming the most important part of my life.

Introduction

HOW DO OTHER gay couples do it? While I was exploring ways to find a partner, I got to know many couples who had been together for ten, twenty-five, and even fifty years. Many of these couples met before Stonewall. Others met post-Stonewall, but their cities and towns were pre-Stonewall, and these men found each other and stayed together in spite of obstacles. The bravest example was a couple I met when I lived in Dallas. The two started out by living openly in their art studio—in Omaha, Nebraska, in the 1950s. Forty years later, when I last saw them just before I moved to Los Angeles, they were still together.

This couple, and the many others I knew, showed me that there are many ways to meet a potential partner and have a fulfilling relationship despite sometimes hostile environments. These couples met in every imaginable way: through mutual friends; in bars, bathhouses, stores, coffeehouses, and movie theatres; at weddings, funerals, parties, and fundraisers; around their neighborhoods; and on vacation. Every "where we met" story had at least one unique twist. Even the most similar stories had elements of difference and surprise.

Once these couples settled in, the variations continued. Some couples continued going to bars, other did not. Some became monogamous immediately, others never did. Many couples shut out their friends, others went out in groups. Seeing all these variations made me wonder how gay couples stayed together.

I also wondered how I could be in a long-lasting relationship. I had already become skilled at ways to meet other men and navigate dating and early intimacy; but I still had some learning to do through a series of short-term relationships that lasted anywhere from six months to three years. Each time, I learned more about myself, my choices, and how to be a better person and partner. Everything I learned was put to use when I met the person at a gay fundraiser who would become my partner. Essentially, I had to fit many puzzle pieces together to figure out what worked and what didn't, and I undertook an honest self-exploration that included therapy, self-reflection, self-help books, and advice and observations from friends and family members.

I also found a common thread that starts when you begin the search for someone who's available, meet this person, and get together for the first time. Once past dating, this same thread winds its way into the uncertainty of the early years and through future periods of the relationship. The thread that winds itself through all these times is intimacy. Intimacy is connected to nearly every aspect of finding a partner and maintaining a relationship.

To help my clients, I applied what I had learned personally and professionally about intimacy. I drew upon my education, training, and experience as a marriage and family therapist to improve and enrich couples' relationships. Part of the motivation for writing this book was that I wanted to reach out to greater numbers of gay men.

I was also prompted to do so when I wrote my first book, a work for mental health professionals on how to provide affirmative therapy for lesbians and gay men that enabled me to consider what much of the profession had neglected. Overlooked questions included: What are the actual differences between heterosexual and same-sex relationships? How does coming out and being gay help and hinder closeness? How do two men in a relationship effectively communicate and resolve their differences?

My hope is that by reading this book you will acquire knowledge by looking at relationships from an objective perspective, yet one that is made relevant by personal experience. It is designed to help you develop new insights and discover new tools for a long-term, intimate relationship.

Where did our challenges with relationships as gay men begin? Most of us had to contend with discrimination and the related fear of coming to terms with our sexual orientation. Although there's no normal reaction to growing up in a homophobic family and an unsupportive school environment, it is fairly common to deceive yourself. You probably used various strategies to deny that you were gay. Maybe you had a girlfriend (if your girlfriend turned out to be lesbian, it's no accident). Or perhaps you thought it was a phase. It's even possible you were attracted to men, had sex exclusively with guys, and still didn't think you were gay.

Whether you realized you were gay early on or whether you had to get past the coping strategy of denial, every gay man must take another important step toward acceptance: telling others. In the meantime, from the moment you realized you were gay to the time you informed significant people in your life, you had to survive by hiding your true feelings and activities. As a result, you were forced to become good at the art of omission. You had to answer questions skillfully and you played along when you were asked questions like "Why aren't you going to the prom?" "What are you doing this weekend?" and "Isn't she hot?"

In the time between coming out to yourself and to others, you may have lived in secrecy and shame. You probably felt bad about having to lie, but you needed to protect yourself from harmful emotional, monetary, and even physical consequences. However, living a life that included covering up who you were could have affected your willingness and capacity to risk being close to someone. You had to create protective coping strategies, many of which are adaptive before coming out but become barriers in the realm of relationships.

The other impact has been on your emotional development and the formation of your identity. If you're like most of us, while your heterosexual peers were having "practice" relationships in high school, you were not. When they had their first opportunities to go out with people of the opposite sex (and often failed until those puzzle pieces fit for them), you didn't dare reveal your interest. This led to developmental delays, such as falling in love with your first boyfriend after knowing him for a few weeks, or having your first awkward dates long after leaving high school.

Shame, coping strategies, and delays in developing your identity have a significant influence on relationships, regardless of when you came out. And whether or not you've come out to all the significant people in your life, these influences cannot be separated from your growth as an individual.

One aspect of personal growth is to accept that (1) no two couples have long-term relationships the same way, and (2) as you grow, you will change over time and so will your relationship. That's why throughout the book I tailor approaches for working through challenges to different circumstances and offer options—in the form of tools—to maintain lasting intimacy rather than insist that there's a right way. For example, some couples can make it (quite well) despite rushing into a relationship. I look at the related challenges and how to handle them rather than simply saying, "Don't do that."

You may have read other books on relationships for gay men. This book encourages your personal growth by focusing on how to choose a potential partner, how to be more satisfied in your current relationship, and how to change frustrating relationship patterns. For many of you, the information will represent the final pieces that complete the puzzle of what it takes to have an intimate relationship, whether the pieces are brand new or serve as timely reminders.

If this is your first book on intimacy for gay men, it provides you with a lot of new, useful information, and I hope it inspires you to seek out other resources to take advantage of several perspectives and find additional information on relationships. To keep the momentum going, I offer several resources at the end of the book.

How to Use This Book

Throughout the book, I refer to three couples who are in three different points in their relationships: Meeting, dating, and in a committed relationship. As the book progresses, so do the couples. I created composites of individuals and couples whom I have known personally and professionally and combined them with my own experiences. Therefore, any potentially identifying information has been completely disguised. Here are the three couples you will get to know, along with their major issues.

CASE STUDY: *Jason and Gregory*

Jason has never been in a relationship. He has been going to clubs fairly regularly, but he's grown tired of the bar scene, feels fairly lonely, and wants to find someone. Jason meets Gregory on the Internet, and we watch them meet, date, and transition to a long-term relationship. They get along fairly well, but they must confront issues related to finances, moving in, and Jason's being in recovery from a crystal meth addiction.

CASE STUDY: *Alex and Mark*

Alex and Mark moved in after knowing each other for three months. They didn't realize how different they were until they lived together. As a result, they don't get along and are at odds on many issues. Their specific relationship challenges relate to friendships, Alex's ex-lover, and money. Broader issues relate to trust, control, and using withdrawal and criticism as forms of communication. Because they have so many issues to work out, Alex and Mark appear often throughout the book.

CASE STUDY: *Roberto and David*

Roberto has been in three relationships. The longest one lasted four years. Roberto has learned a lot about relationships and about himself, and he thinks he's figured out how to find a "keeper." He and David have been together for a couple of years, but David is just now coming out of the closet to his family. Other issues that come up for them are spirituality and monogamy.

As you read the chapters, you'll see "Red Flags" and "Exercises." Red Flags are designed to explore issues and behaviors that you may want to consider avoiding. When you see a Red Flag, you'll be encouraged to think about how it affects you and whether it's something worth continuing, as well as the costs of doing so. Exercises are designed to help you remove roadblocks from your goal of a fulfilling relationship and to progress toward authenticity and intimacy. You may want to keep a journal nearby to jot down ideas, do the exercises, and record your thoughts, feelings, and insights.

For those of you already in a relationship, this book could help you strengthen your connection, give your relationship a more solid foundation, and put an end to ongoing fights and stalemates. For those of you who have had a few short-term relationships, this book offers you ways to see them as "training relationships," to turn your past mistakes into future successes, and to use the tools that will help you navigate your next relationship. If you have not had a serious relationship, this book can help you proceed from the moment you meet someone. In the process, you will learn about yourself and the world of relationships. You'll be ready when an opportunity appears.

You should feel good about picking up this book and deciding to read it. It means that you're taking responsibility for finding lasting intimacy. You're willing to use this book as a guide as you look to yourself for the answers. Taking these steps requires determination and courage, and because both of these are essential ingredients for intimacy, you're on your way.

CHAPTER 1

Gay Men and Intimacy

"INTIMACY" IS A loaded word for gay men. As children and adolescents, we were supposed to learn how to become comfortable with intimacy. Yet most of us had to protect ourselves by hiding our identities from caregivers and other family members who were unfamiliar with what it means to be gay. Self-protection is one of the biggest obstacles to intimacy; therefore, we have to unlearn our natural self-protective reactions as we move out of our comfort zones and become intimate with another man.

If you're single and want to be in an intimate relationship, or if you're currently in one and want to get closer to your partner, it's important for us to have a shared meaning for the word "intimacy." So that we have a common understanding, I have shaped a working definition.

A Definition of Intimacy

Intimacy is an expansive process in which two people grow closer, become supportive of each other, and show compassion through increasing levels of connection and acceptance.

This definition has several components. First, what do I mean by the term "process"? Experiences are what actually happen, and the process is how these experiences occur and the way a relationship grows. Through the process of developing intimacy, you learn to accept your partner's imperfections, find compassion for his problems and weaknesses, work through disagreements, forgive, and grow as individuals and as a couple. The process also includes accepting the natural ebb and flow of emotional closeness and distance.

How does the term "increasing levels" apply? As you share experiences and create a history with someone, you get to know him on a deeper level, even as he is growing and changing as an individual. You accept that your relationship changes as you and your partner change.

How are the terms "connection" and "acceptance" related to intimacy? Connection is the bond; acceptance is letting go of how you think your partner should be. Although two people can know each other for a short time and feel connected, they become much more connected when, through several years of shared history, they have learned to accept each other. In turn, each person's increasing level of acceptance enhances the connection. Consider the following areas in the context of a budding relationship:

- *Sharing personal information*
- *Sensitive areas*
- *Vulnerability and trust*
- *Caring and respect*

Sharing Personal Information

The first time you meet someone and disclose the first small piece of information about yourself, you have begun the process of building intimacy. As you share more information, the other person should also be opening up to you; in this way, you both create the potential for a balanced, reciprocal relationship. Over time, disclosures become more personal. We'll consider this aspect of the relationship as we look at how Jason and Gregory get to know each other.

CASE STUDY: *Jason and Gregory*

Jason is twenty-eight, and he has never been in a relationship. He started looking for a relationship about a year ago. He tried various ways of meeting men, including the Internet, where he met Gregory. They started exchanging e-mails. In one e-mail, Jason mentioned a movie he saw and a hike he recently took. Gregory replied that he hasn't seen the movie but it's on his list. He said that he likes to hike too, but he doesn't like heights, so he has never been on the hike Jason mentioned.

In his next e-mail, Jason asked Gregory what part of the city he lives in. Gregory wrote back telling him his age (thirty) and the neighborhood he lives in, which happens to be an exclusive area. Jason responded that he can't live in that area because the apartments are too expensive. Gregory wrote back and mentioned that he is only able to live there because he got a good deal on his apartment. He also said that he is in the process of buying a home in a more affordable part of town. Gregory mentioned these things because he didn't want to give Jason the impression that he's wealthy, and Jason realized this by reading between the lines.

In the last two e-mails, Jason and Gregory are indirectly disclosing information about their finances, which is a personal area. They still don't know much about each other's financial situation, but they both reveal that they aren't wealthy. Gregory also discloses personal information about his fear of heights, which I'll discuss a bit later.

How do you feel about sharing personal aspects of your life? Let's say that as a child you received negative messages about gay men. As you grew up, you probably felt unprotected and perhaps betrayed by members of your family. When this happens, it's not unusual to have difficulty trusting people. What concerns you about revealing personal information? Can you open up about your trust issues with a future partner?

Feeling bad about certain parts of yourself or past experiences with your family and being reluctant to reveal them can lead to attempts at covering them up as an adult. When you feel the need to cover up personal issues, intimacy becomes riskier for you, and you will find ways to protect yourself.

A related challenge to intimacy for gay men stems from our experiences prior to coming out of the closet. Unfortunately, not only our families but society wanted us to hide, and therefore lie, about our sexual orientation. Pressure to hide came from work, religion and places of worship, schools, and the government. Many of us became very good at hiding or protecting this information about ourselves, but this coping strategy can work against us when we want to become closer to someone and we don't know how to bring down the walls.

Sensitive Areas

We all have sensitive areas: Family members who we wish were different, ways we judge ourselves that are unsympathetic or critical, and things we did that we wish we hadn't. These areas can result in shame and guilt. In small amounts, they are useful because they keep us from indiscriminately hurting others and ourselves. Shame and guilt are different: A person who is ashamed thinks he's bad, defective, or inferior; whereas a guilty person feels sorry about what he has done in the past. Sometimes with shame and guilt, one leads to the other.

Personal information you feel embarrassed or ashamed about can clash with your desire to enter a relationship. For example, if you have occasional problems maintaining an erection, are you willing to talk about it with a potential partner? If not, you see this situation as shameful. Sometimes, however, it's more difficult to be aware of certain areas of shame. But you can get to it by thinking about the way you "talk" to yourself. You may silently kick yourself when you make a mistake, feel you don't fit in, call yourself stupid, idiotic, and pathetic; or you may wonder: What does he see in me?

This self-talk translates into everyday life by not being happy with your body, not venturing opinions because you are afraid of being put down, or feeling bad about a type of sexual activity you enjoy. If the shame is too large, you'd be unwilling to risk talking about personal subjects. Areas of shame need to be small enough so that you feel good about yourself and are willing to share potentially embarrassing information as you and another person get to know each other.

Feelings of guilt also interfere with the desire to be in an intimate relationship. On one end of the spectrum, some people become "apologists." They feel bad about any action that might have even the slightest possibility of hurting someone's feelings. If you have trouble being yourself, perhaps you're afraid of hurting other people or letting them down. Taken together, if you are hiding your past experiences and refuse to let other people know what you're feeling, you may have to overcome the belief that deep down you're not worthy of being in a loving, mutually respectful relationship. Let's look at an exercise to reduce feelings of shame and guilt.

★ EXERCISE: REDUCING FEELINGS OF SHAME AND GUILT

Consider finishing this sentence: "If people really knew me they'd believe that . . . " Think about your traits or experiences and those of your family of origin that you don't want other people to know. Examples of traits include believing that you're not good enough, that you're defective in some way, or unintelligent. Experiences include recurring depression, an addiction or a compulsion, being abused while you were growing up, parents who have had multiple marriages, and racist/homophobic family members. Write about your reactions.

What are your answers? What are the reasons you don't want other people to know about you or your past? Reasons may include concern about being judged and fear of rejection. If you have several shameful areas, it's likely that either you find it difficult to risk rejection or you are afraid that a future partner will use this information against you. But the risk of not revealing them is that they become secrets. And keeping secrets generates a power that produces more shame and gives rise to unhealthy coping strategies. For example, you may become defensive and avoid certain issues, or you may not allow particular discussions to take place. Protectiveness thus gives more energy to these secrets, and shame is more powerful when you won't admit their existence.

If you are the adult child of an alcoholic/drug addict, or if you were raised in a home in which domestic violence or abuse were common, these concerns will come up throughout your relationship. Certain emotional wounds never completely heal, so your only choice is to talk about your experiences, along with your pain and fears, and take the risk with someone who is emotionally supportive. When you grow close to someone, you will eventually want him to know about your personal life and much of your past. When you're willing to open up to others about personal aspects of your life, you're prepared to risk intimacy. Revealing these areas of shame may be the only way to help your potential partner make sense of your fears of abandonment, problems with sex or touch, or reluctance to trust him.

It is risky to reveal unpleasant, shameful, or embarrassing personal information, but your past shaped you into the person you have become; and if you want to grow close to someone, he has to know who you are. How does disclosing shameful aspects of yourself build intimacy? By telling your partner about yourself, you allow him to get to know you better and you offer him the same opportunity for self-disclosure. When he knows that you won't use the information against him, and you feel the same way, you are creating a sense of safety. You'll feel more accepted and connected to one another.

It can be difficult to gauge how much personal information to share and when to share it. For example, talking about an abusive ex-boyfriend in the first few dates may be too soon. You may want to use a need-to-know basis for personal information of this nature. His need to know isn't necessary until the issue starts to emerge in your relationship with him. You can let him know when you feel sure he can be sensitive to the past experiences that cause you to feel distress or anguish.

Likewise, it's important for you to be aware of another person's sharing too much, too soon. You might momentarily cringe when you feel he has stepped over a line. When you feel that, it's okay to mention your discomfort. Sharing your reaction is another opportunity for the two of you to get closer.

Vulnerability and Trust

When you share personal information with another person, you become vulnerable. No one wants to be hurt or rejected, and it is natural to try to avoid it. Being vulnerable is even more challenging if you have been hurt or betrayed in a previous relationship. Allowing yourself to be vulnerable to another person means letting go of the reflexive reaction to protect yourself, which can feel counterintuitive.

Vulnerability requires trust and courage. The more vulnerable you become, the more you have to trust another person. It takes courage to risk vulnerability, but overcoming your fears of disclosing personal information makes you stronger. Let's look at different kinds of trust and how they pertain to intimacy. They include:

- *Keeping confidences*
- *Holding sensitive areas in esteem*
- *Honesty*
- *Dependability*
- *Relationship permanence*

KEEPING CONFIDENCES When you confide in someone, you learn whether you can trust that person to keep your personal information confidential. Your partner should want to keep your private information to himself. If he does keep your confidences, you learn that you can trust him with more sensitive information. As you reveal more about yourself, he should be doing the same and begin trusting that you are also keeping his private information to yourself.

HOLDING SENSITIVE AREAS IN ESTEEM When you reveal embarrassing or painful parts of your life to your partner, you open yourself up to the possibility that he will judge you, use the information as a weapon, or hold it against you. As mentioned earlier, when Jason and Gregory mentioned in their e-mails that

7

they liked to hike, Gregory took a risk when he told Jason that he doesn't hike in a particular area because he's afraid of heights. Many people don't understand the nature of phobias, so he risked opening himself up to ridicule. Gregory hoped he could trust Jason not to minimize his fear of heights or try to convince him to hike in areas that would make him feel vulnerable. If Jason did either of these things, Gregory would feel embarrassed. So Gregory is already placing his trust in Jason.

HONESTY This is a tricky area because to develop feelings of intimacy, you need to be honest without being brutal. For example, let's say that after a few dates you go shopping together. You're both trying on clothes and he shows you a shirt he likes. He'd probably prefer to hear you say that the shirt doesn't suit him rather than tell him that it looks awful. At the same time, you want to show him that you care enough about him to be honest. You wouldn't want to tell him the shirt looks good on him when it doesn't.

DEPENDABILITY You want your partner to know that you will keep your word, and you would expect the same from him. In general, you want to be reliable and consistent. For example, a potential partner will learn that you are dependable when you are on time for dates and never stand him up.

RELATIONSHIP PERMANENCE Once you have developed a bond and learned to accept each other, you and your partner need to trust that you both intend to stay in the relationship, even when it gets rocky. This type of trust is fundamental to allowing a relationship to continue. But if you have a strong fear of being abandoned, you may find it difficult to risk entering a relationship or staying in one. As you become stronger through self-discovery, you'll tolerate rocky and uncertain periods.

Caring and Respect

As you learn to trust each other and become more vulnerable, you will become more intimate and thus care more deeply about each other. You show a partner how much you care by considering his needs and sometimes putting his needs above yours.

One aspect of caring about a prospective partner is to take an interest in his life by paying attention to what he does for a living, asking about his hobbies, and showing respect for his personal background. Respect is closely related to caring. In the context of building intimacy, respect involves being considerate of the other person. When you respect someone, you accept his views, opinions, and feelings even when you strongly disagree. You can have different views on issues such as politics and spirituality, but you have a better chance of growing closer when you respect each other's views. For example, let's say that in your family, it was okay to tell each other what to do; indeed, you're used to this type of behavior. But what if the person you're dating doesn't like to be told what to do? To show respect, you would ask him to do something, not tell him to do it.

But caring and respect for the other person is only half the equation. The other half is caring about and respecting yourself. When you hold yourself in high regard, you expect your partner to respect you, to feel secure despite your different points of view, and to speak up when you are feeling hurt, frustrated, or angry about something he has done.

As you share personal information, you are vulnerable to someone else's perceptions and judgments. You can respond to your own feelings of vulnerability in various ways, and your feelings are influenced by how he reacts. When he consistently offers caring, nonjudgmental reactions, you feel more trusting. As a result of learning that he won't violate your trust, you can feel sure that he cares about you. Respect emerges from caring about each other. Although understanding intimacy and its many aspects is the starting point to being available for an intimate relationship, your availability also depends on how well you know yourself, and this is the next area we consider.

Putting It Together

Intimacy grows as you and your partner become closer, supportive, and caring through a sense of connection and mutual acceptance. It all begins with sharing personal information while allowing yourself to be open and vulnerable. Now that we have looked at intimacy through a gay lens, we build on these ideas in the next chapter by focusing on your readiness for a relationship; this includes helping you determine how your self-image and the way you come across to others influence your ability to be intimate. Readiness also means clarifying your values and preferences and deciding which ones are important in a partner.

CHAPTER 2

Getting Ready for a Relationship

YOU MAY BELIEVE you are ready for intimacy because you desire to be in a relationship; but desiring to be in an intimate relationship isn't the same thing as being available for one. Understanding who you are, clarifying your values, and knowing what you want in a partner all affect your capacity for intimacy. Let's talk about how ready you are and how you can increase your availability.

What's Inside of You?

Imagine that you're carrying a suitcase. Inside the suitcase, you see three compartments. In the first compartment, you harbor fears about intimacy based on experiences with former partners. For example, your ex cheated on you, so you enter prospective relationships with trust issues. A broader issue might be that you distrust people in general; therefore, whether someone cheated on you or not, your lack of trust translates into a tendency to ask a lot of questions, to be skeptical, and to doubt.

The second compartment contains the experiences you had with your family when you were growing up. If you were raised in a dysfunctional family, for example, you may have witnessed fighting throughout your childhood, including outbursts of rage. You may have been aware of things that you should never have known about, such as problems your parents had with each other. This kind of upbringing can make intimacy look dangerous, dramatic, or smothering. Ironically, it can look just as scary if you were raised in a home where honest communication and sharing feelings were not allowed. If you were raised in a home like this, it probably felt as if several individuals were living under one roof, not like a real family, and the thought of being yourself may seem risky.

The third compartment of your suitcase holds experiences you have had with friends, at school, and at work. Although some experiences were positive, others might bring back memories so traumatic that you are reluctant to let down your guard. For example, you may have been teased, taunted, or even beaten up for being perceived as gay. Perhaps you had school friends who revealed your secret or had coworkers who went behind your back.

These three compartments are the sum total of your experiences, and the exterior of the suitcase represents your attitude, perception, and beliefs as a result of your experiences. All three compartments have considerable influence on how you approach dating and relationships. We all come into new situations with varying degrees of trust, hurt from the past, and willingness to risk being with a new person.

Once you realize that you and your suitcase play an important role in finding and sustaining an intimate relationship, you have made progress toward being ready. Because you are willing to discover how your perceptions influence your capacity for intimacy, or availability, you are taking responsibility for removing those barriers. Knowing yourself, which includes clarifying your values and preferences, as well as learning how you come across to others, is key to intimacy.

Coming Out and Relationship Readiness

If you are not yet out to your family and friends, you will face additional challenges in a relationship. For example, you may feel you need to hide the relationship by maintaining a two-bedroom apartment, calling yourselves roommates, or asking your partner to lie for you. Do you recall the lengths the lovers went to in *The Birdcage* (or *La Cage aux Folles*) to hide their twenty-five-year relationship for the sake of their son's wedding? In real life, the result would not be humorous, but the deceit and loss of self-respect would be right on target.

To come out is to tell the truth about yourself while facing the possibility of enormous rejection. What a scary prospect! That's why overcoming your fears by coming out allows you to reveal other aspects of yourself to a potential partner and, in doing so, to become more available.

⁙⁙⁙

You may find it difficult to know who you are and what makes you tick, but it is essential for intimacy. For example, because of society's oppression of gay men, you may have felt compelled to adopt a form of self-protection by hiding your sexual orientation from your family, your friends, the culture at large, and even yourself. There's a good chance that in hiding this part of yourself, you were not fully able to explore who you are and fully develop your identity. To help you consider your identity development, let's take a look at:

- *Your value system*
- *Preferences*
- *How you come across to others*

Your Value System

Your value system consists of the rules and morals you live by. You are aware of many of them. However, some of your values operate outside your awareness. As you hone in on your value system, you increase your readiness for an intimate relationship.

From the moment you meet someone, you are expressing your

values. For example, when you meet someone on the Internet, you can be honest about what you look like by e-mailing a recent photo. Or you could send a photo that's a few years old and hope he will overlook the discrepancy when he meets you in person. Each of these decisions expresses different values. The first decision presents an honest picture, whereas the second decision is slightly dishonest.

Your values influence your actions, but they may not determine them. A sharp contrast between what you believe in and what you do creates internal conflict, which, in turn, causes you to send out mixed signals. For instance, you may value honesty and yet not tell others the truth in certain circumstances, such as when you think the truth would hurt them. But when you do it repeatedly and people realize what you're doing, they learn not to trust your word. Being clear about your values and acting consistently shows a greater readiness for intimacy. And the values you want in a potential partner should be similar to those you hold yourself.

Preferences

When you first meet someone, you might say to your friends, "We have so much in common," or "We talked on the phone for hours." What you're really saying is that you have similar preferences. For example, you like to go to concerts, prefer comedies to action films, or enjoy participating in certain sports. Discussions about your shared interests provide part of the foundation for intimacy.

Sometimes your preferences reflect your values. In fact, a preference can be partly value and partly liking. For example, you may prefer to wake up early in the morning. The next question is: Do you like getting up early because you have a need for accomplishment? Perhaps you're driven and want to succeed in your career, so you get an early start to be productive. The desire to get up early is a preference. The desire to succeed is a value.

The following exercise sheds some light on your values and preferences and sets the tone for compatibility.

★ EXERCISE: VALUES AND PREFERENCES

Within each of the following categories, consider which statement best reflects your views. When none of the choices matches your point of view in a particular category, create your own statement.

The first three categories consist of core values. You want to be with a partner who shares your basic value system rather than with someone who holds different core values but who, you hope, will change. The rest of the categories are preferences. Your values may relate to them, which depends on the importance you place on each particular preference.

1) Honesty

    a. I am honest in every situation, even when I hurt others. Sometimes, people say I'm too honest.

    b. I am generally honest. I am willing to withhold information to avoid uncomfortable situations.

    c. I'm neither extremely honest nor dishonest. I have lied to get out of tight situations, and I think it's okay to stretch the truth under some circumstances.

    d. I don't want other people to know the truth about me or my activities, so either I will not tell them or I will deceive them.

2) Trust

    a. Other people have learned to trust me because I have earned their trust.

    b. I am normally trustworthy, but if other people knew about some of my actions, they might think twice.

    c. I'm usually okay about trust, but I think other people sometimes deserve to be treated poorly.

    d. I betray people's confidences and generally don't care whether people trust me or not.

3) Respect
   a. I have the utmost respect for other people's points of view and their right to live the way they choose.
   b. I have trouble with certain people in my life. I wish they were different.
   c. I tend not to respect other people's beliefs and wishes simply because I usually know better.
   d. If people would do exactly what I want then to do, the world would be a better place.

4) Monogamy
   a. When I get into a relationship, I will have sex only with my partner, and I expect the same from him.
   b. I'm basically monogamous, but I know myself well enough to know I'll have occasional slips.
   c. I'm not into monogamy, but when my partner and I have sex with people, we should impose rules.
   d. Being faithful is an outdated heterosexual notion that doesn't apply to relationships between men.

5) Finances and Saving Money
   a. I save money and hate to spend it on much of anything. Primarily, I am saving for the future.
   b. I balance the present with the future. I like to spend money on nice furniture, a good car, and going out for dinner sometimes, but it's important to save.
   c. I prefer to live for today. While I'm saving some money, I enjoy spending it.
   d. I don't like to look at my credit card balances because they're maxed out. Save money? Are you kidding me?

6) Professional Goals
   a. I live to work. I'm goal-directed, and I want a partner who is

hard working and dedicated.

b. Even though I'm ambitious, a partner's career and career goals wouldn't be important to me.

c. I am not particularly goal-oriented and I hope to find a partner who can help me become more motivated.

d. I work to live and could never be with someone who is driven.

7) Spirituality

a. I am a religious person. I need to go to my place of worship regularly, and I want a partner to go to the same place and have the same beliefs.

b. I have my own spiritual practice. It would be okay for us to express our spirituality differently.

c. I'm not spiritual, but it wouldn't matter whether my partner is or not.

d. I'm not spiritual, and it's important for me to find a nonbeliever.

8) Being Sociable

a. I like being around people. My partner should want to go out with me.

b. I like being around people, but I want a lot of time for just the two of us.

c. I have a couple of close friends, but I expect the two of us to be together by ourselves most of the time.

d. A partner is your only true friend, so I would spend all my time with him.

9) Cleanliness

a. My place needs to look perfect. No clothes lying around and no dishes in the sink.

b. I can handle clutter, but the place needs to be clean (no dirt or dust).

   c. I can handle dirt but the place needs to look neat.

   d. I don't care about dirty clothes lying around or dishes in the sink. I ignore dust build-up and hope someday it eventually stops growing.

10) Adopting or Conceiving

   a. I definitely want kids.

   b. I prefer to have children, but it's not at the top of my list.

   c. Children aren't a priority, but if a future partner wants them, I'd go along.

   d. No way.

11) Having a Routine

   a. I'm habitual. As an example, I always go to the same restaurant and I order the same dish every time.

   b. I'm not entirely into routine. Surprises don't bother me, but it's difficult when I'm thrown off course.

   c. I like routine, but I like spontaneity, too.

   d. I enjoy spontaneity and thrive on new experiences and unpredictability.

12) Alone Time

   a. I want to be alone most of the time.

   b. I like my own company and need an hour or two to rejuvenate. Maybe take an occasional walk by myself or read a book.

   c. It's not important to be by myself. I would much rather be around people.

   d. I hate it when I'm alone and I need to be around others.

Take a look at your answers. The statements that most accurately reflect your values and preferences are your *relationship vision*. Although you can't line up completely with another person, your vision should be similar to your future partner's. This is especially true for the first three items, which comprise your core values. As long as you both have a similarly high regard for honesty, trust, and respect, your relationship readiness will depend on your willingness to tolerate being on opposite ends of the spectrum in a couple of preferences and having one or two degrees of separation in a few others.

How You Come Across to Others

Getting to know yourself includes being aware of how others perceive you. There are two main reasons for discrepancies between how you think you come across to others and how other people see you. One is that you reveal aspects of yourself, including some you may not know about, to others through your actions. Another is that, because communication is complex, your message doesn't always match what you say. An example of this discrepancy is when someone is shy. A shy person knows he is apprehensive or fearful in new situations. Unfortunately, because he is quiet, he can come across as judgmental, standoffish, or snobby. People may not warm up to him because of their perceptions of him; this, in turn, reinforces his fear of meeting new people or starting conversations with strangers.

Because we're often unaware of how we come across to others, we need to listen to what others say to us about our behavior. When several people tell you about a difficulty they're having with you, consider it to be the truth and examine it seriously. Sometimes it's difficult to hear the truth, especially if you are a perfectionist. Remember, though, everyone has flaws, but that doesn't make you a bad person. For instance, if you come across as cold or uncaring, chances are you have your walls up for a reason. As you work through your personal issues, think about the price you're paying for being walled off. Decide to make your actions more closely match your intent. As you do so, you will become more available.

Knowing how you come across to others increases intimacy readiness.

Your capacity for intimacy grows when you develop the courage to learn how other people perceive you. This openness to feedback from others includes positive things they might say about you. When someone offers you a compliment or extols one of your virtues, be willing to take it in by offering a straightforward "thank you."

Getting to know yourself involves being clear about your values and preferences, as well as learning how you come across to others. Each of these processes is about developing your identity; as you know yourself and close the gap between how you see yourself and how others see you, you're more ready for intimacy. This next exercise is an opportunity for you to look at the various beliefs you hold about relationships, which in turn can also help you with readiness.

★ EXERCISE: RELATIONSHIP READINESS

Rate the following items as either Agree (A), Neutral (N), or Disagree (D).

1. *I don't need a partner to be happy.*
2. *I am willing to discuss sex and my HIV status on the first few dates.*
3. *Gay men can't be in a committed relationship.*
4. *I don't really trust people.*
5. *Rejection is not a problem for me.*
6. *When I go out with someone, I need to look perfect.*
7. *I have a fetish, but I never talk about it.*
8. *I am basically secure.*

1. I don't need a partner to be happy.

It's one thing to feel lonely occasionally and to believe that your quality of life would improve if you were in a relationship; it's another matter altogether to believe that you *must* be in a relationship to be happy. The irony is that if you disagree with this statement, you're not as available. When you're needy, you are looking for something outside of yourself to feel complete, maybe to be rescued. When you feel incomplete, no amount of love and attention can substitute for what must come from inside you.

To be ready for a relationship, you must be able to tolerate the natural fluctuations of emotional closeness and distance. There's no greater loneliness than lying next to your partner and feeling all alone. Being unable to tolerate periods of distance places extraordinary demands on a relationship; eventually, the strain can take it to the breaking point.

In contrast, when you feel fairly comfortable with your everyday life and don't mind being alone, you're more ready. To prepare, you must work on yourself. If you're insecure, immature, or needy, explore where these feelings come from so that you can change. Most likely, they relate to unresolved issues from your family of origin. Begin a period of self-exploration to strengthen the relationship you have with yourself. Talk with close friends, see a therapist, read books on personal growth, and keep a journal or blog. Keep the conversations going and you will get to know, respect, and love yourself, which is what it takes to be in a healthy, intimate relationship.

If you need to be in a relationship, you aren't available. On the other hand, if you're fairly comfortable with your life and don't mind being alone, you are.

---

2. I am willing to discuss sex and my HIV status on the first few dates.

If you are HIV-negative, you're probably concerned about contracting HIV. Marking "Agree" or "Neutral" leads to thinking about when to discuss your needs and concerns. Some people think that discussing sex takes the fun out of being spontaneous. What you lose in spontaneity, you gain in the chance to talk openly to the person you're going out with. Discussing HIV may even open the door to talking about your sexual interests and fantasies. Your overtures to talk may be met with resistance, but don't let another person's hesitancy to talk about it derail you. In fact, you can use his reaction as a way to learn more about the person you're dating.

If you have HIV or another chronic sexually transmitted disease (STD), such as herpes or hepatitis, you may be concerned about spreading it. You may also fear rejection. Timing your disclosure can be challenging. You may want to wait to disclose your condition until after a new partner has gotten to know you. Wait too long and you risk his becoming angry or disappointed because you didn't disclose earlier. How long is too long? For some men, after the first kiss is too long. For others, too long is waiting until after two or three dates. Experiment with the timing to discover what is comfortable for you as you attend to the other person's feelings.

A lot of gay men want to get the disclosure out of the way so that they don't waste their time. Actually, getting it out of the way can be a defense against rejection. You aren't giving the other person a chance to make a decision based on his knowledge of you as a person with a condition rather than as a stranger with one. This approach makes it harder for him to reject you out of hand.

Some HIV-positive men will go out only with others who are positive; and, although it's less prevalent than several years ago, some HIV-negative men only consider dating men who are negative. Should you close off your options or be open to going out with men who are the opposite sero-status? As you expand your options and are willing to voice your fears from either side, you add to your readiness.

3. Gay men can't be in a committed relationship.

Many gay men believe that other gay men can't be in a long-term relationship. We can't get married, so it's easier to leave when the going gets rough. It's true that if you live in a place that has no legal ties, it's less messy to end a same-sex relationship. However, you're omitting the many reasons couples stay together whether or not they get married. You're also perhaps not recalling that there are many ways to become legally connected without the institution of marriage: buying a home together, having children, and drawing up wills and powers of attorney.

If you believe that gay men by nature are promiscuous and are not "made" to have a long-term partner, you may be buying into a myth that society has about us and internalizing society's homophobia. While coming out, many gay men have anonymous sex because they would feel threatened if someone they know should find out about their sexual orientation. They require secrecy, so they go to the baths or find other public spaces. After coming out, some gay men go through a candy-store phase because of the liberated feeling that being out brings.

But it's also true that some gay men skip having anonymous sex when they come out and look for a monogamous relationship right away. I have known gay men who were virgins until their twenties and even their thirties. Somewhere in the middle of the extremes, most gay men (just like our counterparts, straight men) have a number of partners before they are ready to settle down. In any case, you have come to the conclusion that you want to be in a committed relationship. Other gay men, whether they have had a large number of anonymous encounters or not, have come to the same conclusion.

||||||||||||||||||||||||||||||||||||||||||||||||||||||||||||||||||||||||||||||||||||||||||||||||||||||||||||||||||||||||||||||||||||||

If you believe that gay men cannot be in a long-term relationship, it comes from buying into society's homophobic beliefs.

||||||||||||||||||||||||||||||||||||||||||||||||||||||||||||||||||||||||||||||||||||||||||||||||||||||||||||||||||||||||||||||||||||||

4. I don't really trust people.

Coming from a substance-abusing family or one that was physically or emotionally abusive affects your ability to trust others as an adult. However, you need not have been raised in these kinds of families to be distrustful. You might have learned not to trust other people if you grew up in a family in which being gay was considered sinful or immoral. Problems with trust can also come from classmates who ostracized you, called you names, or beat you up for being gay. Your sense of trust can also erode by being in a relationship where you were betrayed or had a nasty breakup. In any of these cases, you naturally become leery of others, and if you agreed with this statement, you must learn to trust others so that you can delve (back) into the world of relationships.

You learn to trust someone in one of two ways. One way is to start out fully trusting and see whether he remains trustworthy by gathering information through observing his words and actions. A person who starts off fully trusting of others risks being disappointed or betrayed. The other way, which can be helpful when you begin a new relationship, is to start out by assuming that you don't know whether you can trust this person. Then, he earns your trust as you share experiences. It might take you months or years to trust someone fully. Perhaps what will work best for you is starting a new relationship somewhere in the middle, neither fully trusting nor fully untrusting.

5. Rejection is not a problem for me.

Your ability to withstand rejection is a large part of relationship readiness. When you ask someone out for a cup of coffee or to dinner, you risk being rejected, embarrassed, and stung. Whether or not his rejection has something to do with you, it is natural to take it personally. As you continue to go out with someone, the risk gets higher because as you become more emotionally invested in the other person, you have more to lose.

There are different degrees of being able to tolerate rejection. It's not black or white. Disagreeing with this statement may mean you can handle being rejected, but in small doses. If you fully disagree, you most likely will have to place yourself in situations where you will be asked out until you build up the courage to take "No" for an answer. To handle greater amounts of rejection, take smaller risks first. For example, the anonymity of the Internet could provide you with a starting point. You may have to put yourself out there in small ways and take increasingly larger risks.

6. In order to go out with someone, I need to look perfect.

Agreeing with this statement may mean that you are buying into the standards that have been established by images of how gay men are supposed to look. For example, when you look at TV, newspaper, and billboard advertisements, you tend to see beefy, sculpted men, whether the advertisers are selling medication, cars, or sex.

Over time, the ideal gay body has changed, but when you think about it, as long as there has been a gay community there has been an ideal. Why is that? One answer is that gay men, like straight women, are trying to attract the dominant gender, men. We create our own false belief, like heterosexual women, that we need to go the extra mile to be attractive.

Taking it to the extreme, you may feel the need to lose five pounds before you can ask someone out. Maybe you have fallen for the myth that only buff and handsome gay men are desirable or have partners. The truth is that a good-looking guy may get more *sexual partners,* but it's not the same as finding a relationship partner. It's okay to want to look your best, but thinking you need to have a great face and body to attract and keep a man can actually interfere with intimacy. In fact, it may be used as an excuse to avoid being hurt or rejected.

If you still agree with the statement that you need to look perfect, go to a public area, such as a mall, where gay couples walk together. You will notice that one or both partners aren't in shape and they're not wearing the most recent hair or clothing styles.

7. I have a fetish but never talk about it.

When you start dating, you will want to find out whether you are sexually compatible with the other person. If you are into unusual sexual activities or fetishes, take the risk and tell him; that way, you will find out whether he's into it, or at least willing to accept it. An inability to talk about it could mean that you see your fetish as shameful. If you are ashamed of it, attempt to sort out your feelings.

8. I am basically secure.

To find lasting intimacy, you need to be secure enough to handle rejection, have a basic understanding of yourself, and withstand difficult feelings. You must work on yourself enough to risk becoming intimate. If you are basically secure but feel that you need to be totally secure to risk intimacy, don't wait because total security is not achievable.

On the other hand, insecure people compare their insides (thoughts and feelings) to other people's outsides (what they see). They think that secure people have something they lack. Ironically, most insecure individuals haven't learned one of the best-kept secrets: Everyone has areas of weakness and insecurity. Knowing this should make you feel more confident about taking the risk.

Putting It Together

Making yourself available for an intimate relationship begins with knowing yourself. This involves looking at your values and preferences, deciding what's important in a partner, and being willing to tolerate some differences. Becoming available also means learning how you come across to others and questioning long-held beliefs, such as "needing" to be in a relationship and expecting to find intimacy despite having trouble trusting others. When you feel ready, new questions arise about where to meet available men, how to approach them, and what to do on the first few dates.

CHAPTER 3

Meeting and Dating Men

NEARLY ALL OF us have experienced difficulty in finding other men who are ready for a relationship. One important question: How do you increase your chances of meeting available men and asking someone out or being asked out? Then, after the first date, how do you proceed to the second? Let's look at several ways to meet available men and what to expect on the first couple of dates.

Meeting Available Men

You may find meeting available men a challenge. Fortunately, you can take action to maximize the possibility. The more men you meet, the greater the possibility for a connection. So, where do you meet other men? Let's consider the options and weigh the advantages and disadvantages of each one:

- *Mutual friends*
- *Public places*
- *The four Bs (bars, bathhouses, bookstores, and bushes)*
- *The Internet*
- *Political, religious, and social organizations*

Mutual Friends

When mutual friends introduce you to someone, it could bode well because they know your likes and dislikes, temperament, and characteristics as well as his. So there's a good chance you will have a lot in common and get along well. You wouldn't necessarily have to worry that he might be flaky, and you could even be confident that he is looking for a long-term relationship. If your friends don't know him very well, at least they see something in both of you that makes them think you'd hit it off.

Meeting someone through friends can happen in one of three ways. The first two are planned: Either your friends introduce you in person or give you his contact information so that you can meet him for the first time on your own. The third way is through a chance meeting at a social gathering hosted by a mutual friend.

The first way, when friends formally introduce you, can be uncomfortable because your introduction is public and you might feel self-conscious. To reduce potential awkwardness, when your friends tell you that they have someone in mind, you could ask them to refrain from telling him that you're interested. This may lead to a more comfortable experience.

If you both know why you're being introduced to each other, you can still find ways to reduce the possibility of awkward situations. For example, don't feel compelled to exchange phone numbers with him. If you decide you want this person's number, you can call your friends and let them know a day or two later. They can then tell you whether they have talked to him and what he said after meeting you. In the meantime, remember that the initial meeting lasts for just one evening and you're not obligated to go out with him. You can make the best of it by realizing that you may meet a new platonic friend rather than someone to go out with.

Going out by yourselves the first time you meet can feel awkward because no one else is there to help you keep the conversation going or act as a buffer if you don't relate well. However, going out by yourselves has some advantages. For one, you won't be under a public spotlight. If only one of you likes the other, the embarrassment isn't played out in front of friends. And the potential for a romantic feeling could set the tone for future dates.

The third, most casual, way of meeting someone through mutual friends happens without any advance planning. For instance, let's say your friends invite you to a party and you haven't met some of their friends. Among the people you meet, you talk for a while to someone you find interesting. Your meeting is less forced, and no one knows you're talking to him because you're interested in going out with him. Yet you have the earlier mentioned advantage of not needing to exchange phone numbers. You don't even need to ask him out; instead, talk to your friends later and ask whether he's got a boyfriend, or is even looking. Perhaps he mentioned to them he liked meeting you and wanted to know more about you. You can contact him at that time.

Being introduced to someone through mutual friends is an excellent way to meet men. Your willingness to handle the potential awkwardness that comes from this makes meeting someone this way potentially rewarding.

Public Places

You're at a grocery store or the Home Depot in a gay part of town and the two of you check each other out. You're at a movie theatre and spot someone who is alone, or you're at the gym and literally spot someone. You can find opportunities wherever you are. When you take a chance, at least you won't regret not saying hello. It won't be much different whether you're in a gay part of the city (if your city has one). Going to gay spaces reduces the chance you will mistake a heterosexual for a gay man, but, either way, you must ask yourself which is worse: regretting you never took the chance to meet him or feeling bad because he wasn't interested?

To start a conversation with someone, think about the context. You're in a coffee shop; to keep it light, talk to someone about coffee or about the place itself. Let's say you're in line at a locally owned coffee shop. You can say something like, "This line is always long, but I like coming here more than going to the chains." He agrees, and you add that you like their coffee so it's worth the wait.

By then, you'll be able to tell by his response and body language whether he's open to talking or would like to be left alone. You can chat a bit longer, maybe ask a question or two. When he sits down at a table, sit at the table next to his and continue the conversation. Or you might wait until you run into him at the coffee shop the next time.

The advantage of repeatedly going to the same coffee shop is that you see familiar faces and come to recognize them, and they will recognize you. It's much easier to strike up a conversation after the third or fourth time you see someone. And you don't need to restrict friendly overtures only to people you're attracted to; instead, be friendly and open to meeting new people in general.

Avoid clichés, unless you use them with humor or irony. Questions such as "Do you come here a lot?" or "What's your sign?" are clichés, and so are sexual come-ons such as, "I could make better coffee for you first thing in the morning than this place," or the over-used "Don't I know you from somewhere?" Try to be genuine. You can say, "Hi, I'm John Smith." That's it. Then see how he reacts. If he's not interested in going out with you, you will still know a friendly face by name.

The Four Bs: Bars, Bathhouses, Bookstores, and Bushes

You can meet someone at a bar, in a bathhouse, at a bookstore, or in the bushes. But you are unlikely to meet a potential partner in these places because men frequent them principally to look for sex. Nonetheless, it's possible. Think of it this way: You are there, and you want to be in a relationship. Other men at the B-place want to be in one too, and many of them go simply to have their sexual needs met until that time. However, be aware that going exclusively to sexual spaces to find someone can be a trap. You should broaden your scope, go beyond the four Bs, to give yourself more opportunity to find someone with whom you can have a relationship.

―――

Although it's possible to find a partner in one of the four Bs, the odds aren't in your favor.

―――

However, because you're being sexually direct at the four Bs, you can be straightforward with your conversation (even if it's minimal). Let's say you meet someone at a sex club and want to ask him out. To arrange a date, the next step is the same, regardless of where you might meet someone; that is, you would ask him for his phone number or e-mail address and then contact him. During the next conversation, you can talk about when and where to meet again.

Whether you have had sex with him or not, it's possible you won't want to have sex when you meet the next time. If so, let him know that you don't want to have sex because you'd like to get to know him better first. Otherwise, he could easily assume you were turned off by something he said or did during the date.

The Internet

The Internet has become the world's largest dating service. You have advantages by meeting men on the Web, especially if you're shy or introverted. Given the relative anonymity, you can test the waters without meeting men face-to-face. You can learn about someone before going on the first date. Because of the sheer numbers, you're able to meet a lot of men on the Internet and increase your odds of meeting someone who is looking for a serious relationship.

Because the Internet is also the world's largest place to hook up, you can use dating services that pre-screen and validate information among members. Some sites pre-screen and qualify members online and perform the match offline; others do it all online. Some charge right away, but others don't charge you until you have set up your personal profile and you start making contact with other members.

You can choose from among many dating services, so do some research before jumping into the virtual world of dating. You may want to try two or three dating services simultaneously.

Alternatively, place personal ads or answer ads with dating services that don't screen, or go directly to message boards and chat rooms. Although this approach is less costly, your search is more likely to be lengthier because these sites don't screen people and therefore don't filter out those who are insincere, flaky, or a bad match.

The Internet is useful, but it has its drawbacks. The relative anonymity of the Internet can lead some men to create personas out of thin air. Also, some gay men use dating services as a pretense for sex, so try to filter out men who say they are looking for a relationship but are actually looking for sexual partners. The easiest way to focus on relationships is to avoid virtual sexual spaces. Otherwise, when you look at ads or engage in chat, reconsider the men you sense are not seriously looking. You can distinguish between a man who wants to get together right away (tonight) from someone who wants to get to know you by exchanging e-mails or talking first. You can also tell a lot from the tone of the e-mails and phone calls. Someone who overloads his communication with sexual innuendoes is probably not looking for the same thing you are looking for.

Another pitfall is developing e-mail relationships. This kind of relationship usually begins by meeting someone on the Internet (or in person but swapping e-mail addresses) and then not progressing beyond your exchanges of e-mails. The e-mails can feel intimate, but they become a substitute for true intimacy. Because more information is communicated nonverbally than verbally, you miss learning important things about him if you persist too long with e-mails. Only by observing how he behaves can you really learn about him.

Through an e-mail relationship you can get to know someone's secrets, dreams, and fantasies without the fear of progressing to dating or thinking about committing at some point. You can seek out mutual emotional support, but generally not much more. Intimacy includes allowing yourself to be vulnerable and working through fears of being rejected, so an e-mail relationship is much safer than an actual relationship. With little investment, your relationship could literally end with the click of a mouse.

If you feel a connection to someone you meet on the Internet, it's important to inject reality into the situation by meeting him in person before a fantasy of who he is takes over. If you try to meet and he makes excuses not to, you know that you're heading for a virtual relationship.

Despite the challenges of finding a good match, it is quite possible to meet someone with whom you can have a serious relationship on the Internet. You may become frustrated during the process, but don't let your initial experiences diminish your determination. Persistence and patience can pay off.

Political, Religious, and Social Organizations

Working for a political cause, volunteering at a nonprofit organization, attending a fundraiser, and going to a place of worship are opportune ways to meet men. These places lend themselves to meeting potentials because your interests, beliefs, and values will most likely be similar to those of other men who are there. It's relatively easy to start a conversation when you meet someone because you can legitimately talk about what is happening around you. Examples include, "What kinds of things have you done for this organization?" or "How did you start volunteering here?" Notice the questions are open-ended and elicit explanations rather than simple yes or no answers.

The key to meeting people in any of these ways is to attend meetings or services regularly. In the beginning, you may feel like an observer. Over time, you can't help but meet people and talk to them. Talking to other people is often the norm in volunteer work, or else it's a required part of your responsibilities. At places of worship, the social component is important even though people attend for religious reasons. Although looking for a relationship may not be the primary reason you attend a place of worship, be open to meeting other people, including someone to ask out.

When you meet a person in two different contexts, you increase your chances of talking to him and asking him for a date or being asked out. For example, let's say you see a person at a political meeting and later run into him at a grocery store. You could start a conversation at the store by saying you recognize him from the political meeting and take it from there. Or you could simply say hi to him at the grocery store and wait until the next political meeting to talk about the probability that you both live in the same neighborhood or frequent places familiar to both of you.

Dating

Many gay men don't look forward to dating. Mostly, we see it as an unpleasant means to an end. My hope is that you can readjust the lens so that you learn to enjoy the ride as much as the destination and not see it as a waste if your dates don't turn into a relationship. To that end, let's look at ways to make dating more enjoyable and find out how to use the time with someone as a growth experience.

The "Prospect" of Dating

Dating is a form of exploration. When you go out with someone, you are giving yourself the opportunity to learn whether he is someone you want to be in a relationship with, become friends with, just have sex with (a buddy), or no longer see.

The idea that you need to put yourself out there is what's behind organization- and bar-sponsored events such as speed dating, where men spend only a minute or two with other participants, and silent dating, where gay men converse with potential partners through e-mail, handwritten notes, and text messaging. People who run these services understand that you don't need to know someone for very long to determine whether you want to go out with him. However, going out with someone for weeks and months is necessary if you are to move from attraction to learning whether you're compatible and share a similar attitude toward relationships. Also, you have to date for a while before you get to know someone because each person has a multifaceted combination of perspectives and experiences.

The First Date

You have several options for going out the first time. Although e-mailing has become as common as calling, a phone call is more personal. Setting up the first date can rouse a lot of emotions. Each of you builds up interest, expectation, and apprehension. It's natural to be anxious when you're going out for the first time, but try to keep the situation in perspective. Remember you're doing this to start exploring.

Being socialized as a male can come into play here. In heterosexual dating, the initiator is still usually the male. But what about two gay men? Because men are socialized to be aggressors, thinking about setting up the initial date can be confusing. Essentially, who should ask whom out?

To answer this for yourself, try to keep it simple at the beginning. It's okay to state your preference in a way that can easily be understood. For example, if you just say, "Give me a call," you send a message implying that you want to be the one to be contacted. Conversely, "I'll call you" sends the opposite message. You could also wait for him to make a suggestion.

At this point, it's helpful to question your beliefs about what it means to be a man. If you can only be the initiator, are you carrying subconscious beliefs? Sometimes, it's just a preference, but it may be a sign that you have trouble yielding to or accommodating another person. If so, it may be worth looking into, which is what we do in chapter 9.

If you say you'll call him, how soon should you call after meeting him? Contacting him right away carries risks, but so does delaying. Contacting him the same day or the next can appear to be too soon.

On the other hand, you may seem uninterested if you wait a week. Above all, the answer to the question is to be yourself, to be concerned about what you want to do, and to take your lifestyle into account (how busy you are, etc.). It all depends mainly on what you want to do and how connected you feel to him. You don't need to set up the date the very first time you talk to him. You can call or e-mail him later to suggest a place. Second-guessing him or worrying about what he thinks can get you off to a shaky start.

WHERE DO YOU GO? Regardless of how you met, reduce the possibility for discomfort by getting together at a public place. One advantage to meeting somewhere is the possibility of an easy exit if you don't like him. If you're not interested, you can back away more easily than if you're at his place or yours. Plus, when you suggest meeting in a public place, you communicate to him that the date will be focused on getting to know each other.

Where you go on the first date sends a message. You convey a light message, more like getting together than a true date, when you suggest going to a café or a coffee shop. However, if you are shy or not very talkative, you might wonder whether you can sustain a conversation with someone you don't know. In that case, suggest going to a place where you don't have to talk as much, such as a movie, a museum, or an art gallery.

WHAT DO YOU TALK ABOUT? Most people feel comfortable talking about themselves when they meet someone new, so ask him about his hobbies, his work, where he lives, and whether he likes his neighborhood. Just talking about his family background—how many brothers and sisters he has, where they live, and where he grew up—can take a while. Ask him whether he has pets and where he has traveled. Questions are a good way to get to know him and they help advance the conversation.

If you were introduced by friends, you have a natural topic of conversation: them. Another topic is current events. Talking about what's in the news indicates whether he likes to keep up and how much he cares about what's happening. Someone who reads the sports page only is giving you information about his primary interests. Also, make observations about the place you're in and the surrounding area. Note the nearby shops or restaurants and why you like them.

You don't want to ask a nonstop series of questions because you risk sounding like an interviewer. Rather, add comments and occasionally compare his situations to yours. Invite him to talk about himself by saying, for example, "Tell me about your family," or use a simple phrase like "such as" when you want to elicit additional information from him. Even saying the last word of his sentence (called an accent) elicits more information. You eventually want to have a narrative of him and his life, but on the first date you are gaining snapshots only. For example, by finding out what motivated him to pick his occupation, you are beginning to learn about his values. You will get an idea of whether he likes to be around people or prefers to be alone; whether he would like to advance in his career or is content to stay where he is; and whether he puts his career above everything else.

Occasionally follow up a question with a statement. Perhaps you or someone you know is in a similar situation or has had a similar experience. As you share similarities, you are starting to build intimacy, and this will strengthen if he asks you similar questions. He should show some interest in you and your background; if he doesn't, it could be a clue that he's self-centered (alternatively, he could just be talkative or nervous). Generally, topics of mutual interest should flow easily between the two of you.

WHAT SHOULD YOU AVOID? There are only four subjects to avoid on your first date: old boyfriends, previous boyfriends, former boyfriends, and ex boyfriends! It's not a good idea to ask him or bring up the topic of your past relationships until after you have gotten to know each other. Similarly, be judicious about bringing up childhood abuse, depression, and drug history.

Revealing Personal Information

This leads to the question of when to reveal personal information. To begin the discussion, consider Jason and Gregory's first date.

CASE STUDY: *Jason and Gregory*

Jason and Gregory, who have been exchanging e-mails for a few weeks, meet at a restaurant for dinner. When they are seated, the waiter asks whether they want to start with a beer or glass of wine. Jason says he wants a soda, and Gregory orders wine. After the waiter leaves, Gregory asks, "You don't drink?" Jason appears flustered and just smiles weakly. Gregory, trying to prevent further awkwardness, doesn't ask follow-up questions. The topic of drinking doesn't come up again, and the rest of the date proceeds smoothly.

As it turns out, Jason was drinking a lot and using crystal meth and Ecstasy when he was in the club scene. About a year ago, he realized he had developed a crystal addiction. He started going to Narcotics Anonymous and has not used drugs for six months. Because he did have a couple of slips with crystal, and they always started with drinking, he felt he had to eliminate alcohol from his life as well.

Like Jason, when you're faced with a similar question, you could take one of two approaches, or a combination of the two. The first is the need-to-know basis. With this approach, you keep personal information to a minimum. For example, if you're in recovery, you could limit yourself to telling others simply that you don't drink until you feel prepared to reveal why.

You could also mention that you are in recovery, which is the second approach, or the putting-your-cards-on-the-table approach. Recovery is similar to HIV status and other personal information in this regard. But with a cards-on-the-table approach, you still wouldn't have to elaborate about how long you've been in the program, what your drugs of choice were, or anything else related to your recovery.

If you reveal that you're in recovery and he doesn't ask any questions, he'd be showing respect for your privacy. Gregory knew that it was a possible issue for Jason, so he felt he would have been intrusive if he asked questions. However, if you're pressed with additional questions, you might have to let him know that he's delving too far into your personal life. But let's say that the other person is also in recovery and he mentions it on the first date. It would then be okay to touch on the subject but not necessarily to go into it deeply.

The major point is to keep things light. Let's say your date mentions his past, where he was raised, when he came out, and also talks a bit about his kids or nieces and nephews; otherwise, he sticks to current events. If so, he is exhibiting good judgment. "Boundaries" is the word that relates to how much one reveals right away. When someone mentions his parents' nasty divorce, his ADD and bipolar disorder, and the number of men he has had sex with on the first date, his lack of boundaries is cause for concern. Although this is an exaggerated example, plain good judgment is useful, and you should listen for his common sense regarding what he talks about. If you find it challenging to conceptualize boundaries, consider your feelings instead. If you find yourself feeling uncomfortable or cringing from time to time as he talks, he may be overstepping his bounds.

Progressing to the Second Date

Let's say things don't go well and you'd rather not see him again. You can use a blend of the need-to-know and cards-on-the-table approaches. With the first approach, you don't mention going out on a second date. If he doesn't mention it either, you're under no obligation to talk to him again. Should he say, "Let's get together again," let him know you're not interested. Part of being available is tolerating difficult emotions, so if you answer him directly, you are stretching your "courage muscles" by letting him know.

More important, what if you are interested? It's fine to tell him during the date that you want to see him again. In fact, a straightforward approach can lead to a smoother progression to the next one. To illustrate how you could go about this, let's look at the end of Jason and Gregory's first date.

CASE STUDY: *Jason and Gregory*

Jason tells Gregory he had a great time and looks forward to seeing him again. Neither one sets a time or place for the next date. As they're saying goodbye, Gregory says, "I'll give you a call." Jason responds, "Great, and if I don't hear from you by Thursday, I'll send you an e-mail." Jason replies that he will send Gregory an e-mail if he doesn't hear from him so that he can feel a sense of personal control. Responding with "okay" would have meant he'd have to wait for Gregory to call, and he knew he would have grown anxious as the days rolled on.

When you want to go out again, how soon should the next date be? I have heard stories from many gay couples in long-term relationships. Their answers range from "We have been together ever since" to "We saw each other a week or two later." Use the same logic about when to contact him that I mentioned earlier: Focus primarily on what you want rather than anticipating what he wants. However, you gain a better perspective when you start out slowly and take the time to get to know him.

It's fairly common to talk to each other or to exchange e-mails after the first date. Some people keep contact to a minimum, but others talk to each other a lot. There's no right way to go about this, so go with how you feel. If he's calling you every day and you'd rather talk less often, it's okay to tell him that you would prefer to talk once or twice a week while at the same time mentioning how much you look forward to seeing him again. Otherwise, enjoy!

Where do you go for a second date? A few options include going to a play, a movie, a museum, or a concert. People commonly combine going to a movie or play with a meal, and when you go out for lunch or dinner, you learn about him through conversation and how he behaves in public.

Dating is about exploring, so you will gather more information about him as you plan the second date. Be curious about how he behaves toward you as you plan. For example, when you ask him where he wants to go and he responds, "Whatever you decide," is he being considerate or indecisive? On the other hand, if he tells you where he wants to go and doesn't ask for your opinion, is he a decisive person or on the selfish side? You don't have enough information to be able to answer those types of questions, which is where the next few dates and beyond enter the picture.

Putting It Together

You increase your chances of meeting available men by being open to people wherever you happen to be. Different places require that you adapt your approach. For some, the Internet works well; for others, mutual friends or public spaces fit better. The key is to know what's best for you and your preferences.

When you start dating, your time together is a period of exploring compatibility and shared interests. Excitement builds when you learn that the interest is mutual and that you have a lot in common; indeed, when this happens, it is natural that you will enjoy spending time with him. However, it isn't long before you reach the uncharted territory of early intimacy with this new person. Interpreting new experiences and learning how to manage them are the focus of the next chapter.

CHAPTER 4
Early Intimacy

STARTING A NEW relationship and building intimacy involves learning new skills. A lack of a solid foundation and uncertainty are generally the norm at this time; therefore, while keeping your comfort level in mind—and his, too—you must first learn what's going on as the relationship develops and then choose how to proceed.

To begin this process, let's say it's been several weeks since you started dating someone and you want to continue seeing him. You enjoy each other's company, you talk on the phone frequently, and you exchange e-mails; in other words, you spend a great deal of time thinking about him. At the same time, you're beginning to feel pangs of insecurity that could eventually interfere with intimacy. You may feel ambivalent about going forward and wonder how to proceed. Let's talk about early intimacy by considering Jason and Gregory's situation.

CASE STUDY: *Jason and Gregory*

During their fourth date, Jason says he is attracted to Gregory and he's been thinking about having sex with him, except he wants to get to know him better first. He also talks about being HIV negative and his worry about becoming infected.

Jason also purposely withholds certain information from Gregory. For instance, he doesn't reveal that he was abused when he was younger and, as a result, has some issues concerning sex and control, including occasional impotence. He knows that at some point he needs to broach the subject, but he isn't willing to do so yet. Instead, he starts by talking about HIV and wants to settle that issue as well as find out how Gregory reacts to his concerns. He's decided not to reveal this very personal information about his past until he feels ready, which won't happen until they are farther down the road.

Opening the Door to Intimacy

Jason is taking a risk by talking about his attraction to Gregory and revealing his concerns about HIV. Jason sees the disclosures he made as a first step toward broaching more sensitive areas. Nonetheless, Jason offers Gregory enough information to be vulnerable. As Jason is taking this risk, he is letting his guard down and therefore is opening the door to intimacy.

Sociologist Peter Nardi talks about how friends continually reveal increasingly personal information to each other as their relationships deepen. The process of making friends begins in a way similar to that of developing a relationship with a potential partner. As Jason reveals information about himself and as Gregory reciprocates, they feel closer to each other and are taking the first steps toward intimacy.

The First Time

If you have sex right away with someone, you risk creating artificial intimacy. Although you want to have sex with him before the window closes (perhaps when the relationship feels more like a friendship), you have plenty of time to introduce sex into the relationship as you continue to get to know each other.

In addition to opening up the lines of communication by bringing up HIV, Jason wants to hear Gregory's response. Jason knows that he won't be fully trusting of Gregory's answer until he is assured that Gregory's actions match his words when they do have sex, but he wants some validation for his fears. Gregory lets Jason know that he is positive, and quickly adds that he's extremely careful.

The Driver's Seat

By not worrying what Gregory thinks and instead gathering information about Gregory, Jason is staying in the driver's seat. Jason accepts that Gregory is also in the driver's seat at the same time. In other words, Jason places his emphasis on whether Gregory is right for him and is not as concerned about being right for Gregory. When you're dating someone, it's easy to lose perspective. However, staying in the driver's seat means exploring whether the person you're dating is right for you. You are aware of how he's treating you; you notice whether he is reciprocating; and you consider whether he's saying or doing things that concern you.

When you keep the focus on whether he's right for you and not on whether he wants you, you're in the driver's seat.

It may seem selfish to think this way, but you may be doing it in reverse; that is, you might be saying to yourself that you hope he accepts you or that you're right for him. This can cause you to change what you say or do to conform to his personality. It can lead to your trying too hard to please him and to get him to like you, and as a result you are not yourself. A specific way to be in the driver's seat is to consider personal and sensitive areas as litmus tests and to find out whether you are dating someone who is sensitive to your problems and insecurities. For example, Jason only thinks about being with someone who is going to be sensitive to his impotence; he does not worry whether Gregory will accept him with the condition.

Leaving the driver's seat and worrying about whether you're right for him is one way you increase the possibility of hurting the chances for early intimacy to develop. It is also possible that you are harming your chances in other ways. The following Red Flag proposes five ways you could sabotage early intimacy.

RED FLAG: *Five Ways to Self-Sabotage During Early Intimacy*

1. Bring up your ex-boyfriend, how he mistreated you, what a jerk he was, and how horrible he was during your break-up.

Talking about your ex in a bitter or angry way can mean you haven't moved on emotionally. The person you're dating might wonder what kind of person you are, and he might even consider the possibility that you will be talking about him like this someday. On the other hand, as you talk to each other on an intimate level, ex-partners will come up in the conversation. It's okay to share what happened, good and bad.

2. Talk about yourself *a lot,* and don't give him a chance to say much.

If the person you're dating talks incessantly, consequently not showing much interest in you or your life, how would you feel? You may think he is self-centered and probably give up on having a meaningful conversation. On the other hand, you may become talkative when you are nervous, becoming chatty during your dates. But because dating provides snapshots of who you are, the person you're seeing will perceive you as self-centered, regardless of the truth.

3. After the first date, call him and e-mail him a lot, and when he says he's too busy to see you, get upset or pout.

If you won't leave him alone after the first few dates, it could be because you're crazy about him and think he's "The One." However, you run the risk of coming across as clingy, and he might feel like shaking you off. A shy person could be reluctant to tell you that you're coming on too strong and, as a consequence, simply do "the fade." You're left wondering why he won't return your calls or e-mails.

4. Make things into an issue, bring up your differences, and start conversations with statements such as "There's something we need to discuss."

Before dating becomes more serious, few things should be made into an issue. You can simply mention that you don't care for some things without explaining yourself. You can handle things as they come up and not bring them up as issues to be hashed out. If you start bringing up serious concerns early on, you may scare him off.

5. Tell him that if he's not serious about being with you in the future, the two of you should just end it.

Because dating is about exploration, every person you date will not turn into a long-term partner. If at some point you realize that he's not a potential partner, you can still go out together. It is only fair, however, that you tell him that you don't think it's going anywhere. However, you run the risk of coming across as needy or controlling if you tell him that he must be serious about becoming your partner. If you do feel that way, you could be shooting yourself in the foot.

This Red Flag illustrates why it's important to feel fairly complete as a single person. Feeling okay with being alone and at the same time wanting someone in your life will reduce your chances for this kind of self-sabotage. As you relax and see dating as a form of exploration, you are giving the person you're dating the opportunity to like you for who you are. When you feel complete, you are more likely to experience relative ease during early intimacy and have your dates turn into a satisfying, intimate relationship.

Though each of you is wearing your best "dating face," I would still encourage you to strive to be yourself. Let him determine whether you are right for him, and focus on whether he is right for you. Because dating is about exploring, you want to think in terms of compatibility and shared interests. The ultimate question is this: Is he the person I want to be in a relationship with?

Transitioning to a Relationship

This leads us to the topic of the transitional time from dating to a serious relationship. People probably use the word "serious" as a way of describing a deepening relationship because, as intimacy expands, a shift is taking place between two people who are creating a third entity—the relationship—out of two different lives. However, when dating turns serious, which is anywhere from a month to a year or two, several themes emerge.

Trust and vulnerability take center stage. Recall from chapter 1 that there are many kinds of trust. You learn whether you can trust him to be honest with you, whether he is caring, and whether his words are consistent with his actions. If you're not completely out of the closet, you are discovering whether you can trust him not to say anything to people who do not know about your sexual orientation.

Another theme is making future plans, which is a significant way to show your interest. When a special event such as a play or an art exhibit is coming up in a couple of months, ask him whether he'd be interested going. Make future plans for a get-away or a longer trip. Discuss where you want to go, where you'd like to stay, and what you'd like to do. You learn new things about him as you plan the trip, and during the vacation you will learn a lot about how compatible you are.

A third emerging theme is revealing information, including how you feel about certain aspects of the relationship and the relationship itself. Let's say you have been dating someone for six months. You see each other a few times a week and you're falling in love with him. When and how should you bring up the following subjects?

- *Talking about exclusivity*
- *Making plans to meet the family*
- *Discussing the possibility of moving in*

Talking about Exclusivity

In the beginning, you have no reason to tell him whether you're dating other people. Prior to discussing your relationship, one way to broach the subject is to talk about relationships in general and your expectations. You may find you're both the type of person who can date only one person at a time. In this case, you have already answered the question. However, you may differ, and you can discuss exclusivity to learn about him while at the same time working on giving him the freedom to choose what is best for him.

Making Plans to Meet the Family

As your relationship turns serious, your boyfriend will most likely want you to meet his family, and you'll want him to meet yours. If one family lives out of town, a natural time to visit is during a celebration, such as the holidays or a graduation. Or you could decide just to go and meet the family. To consider his needs and feelings, inform him when you feel ready to meet them. If, on the other hand, you're not ready, let him know. You can add that you would like to meet them someday.

Discussing the Possibility of Moving In

When you talk about moving in someday, you are setting the stage for commitment. The talks don't need a particular format, but the needs of both of you should be taken into account. When one of you feels strongly about something—for example, he's between jobs and doesn't want to move until he knows what part of town he will be working in—then the person with the stronger rationale should be considered first.

Sometimes moving in isn't practical. What if you both own your own homes? What if your work places are so far apart that if one of you moved, the commute would be unbearable? Alternatively, what if you simply know that moving in with someone is not an option? Not all couples move in together, but discussions about it or talks about deepening the relationship generally start at about this time.

In regard to all of these emerging themes, listen carefully to his wants and needs, and then voice yours. You shouldn't worry about being interrupted, being put down, or being belittled for your thoughts and feelings. When you discuss serious subjects in a mutually respectful atmosphere, you are increasing the level of intimacy. Discussions and planning are the first true tests of your compatibility. As you focus on these possibilities, get past the tests, and realize that you want to be together, you may experience a honeymoon.

The Honeymoon

You know he is "The One." You can't wait to see him and you spend many hours thinking about him. You focus on your common interests and get along famously. You excitedly tell your friends about him and how wonderful he is. Perhaps he's the "greatest guy in the world." You simply can't get enough of him.

However, you haven't fully gotten to know him. The whole person has not completely come into focus because either you're overlooking his faults, he's on his best behavior, or a combination of the two. There are theories about why this happens, including one that suggests that this phase is the glue that holds couples together when times get rough. During challenging times, each partner can look back at the beginning to remember why they got into the relationship; in doing so, they each hope to return to the time when they were in love.

The honeymoon is akin to infatuation. Though infatuation is a type of intimacy, it's not the same as the kind of intimacy between people who have a shared history, know one another on a deep level, accept each other's faults and shortcomings, and make sure that the relationship is on steady ground.

Still, the honeymoon is an important time, and for many couples, it's an important part of building a relationship. You discover common interests, talk about your future together, and set up sexual roles. You're establishing early intimacy with someone who is becoming your partner. But for the relationship to continue, remember that the feelings cannot be sustained forever.

Not every couple experiences the honeymoon phase. You might take things slowly with the person you're seeing, or you might not feel it at all. There's nothing written that you need to be infatuated with someone you're seeing or that you should see him more than once or twice a week, even after dating for six months or more. What's more important is you tell the person you're seeing what your intentions are. If you tell him that you want to take things slowly, and that you are interested in having a relationship progress without pushing anything, and he agrees, you're developing a strong foundation for the relationship.

Challenges During Early Intimacy

Although we have thus far looked at a forward-moving transition to getting closer, we now turn to some difficulties in moving beyond early intimacy. Part of what happens is that when challenges hit it's hard to figure out what's going on. What is it? How come it happens? What's going "wrong" is part of a learning process, so what's going wrong may actually be what you need so that you can learn about yourself, about dating, and about preparing for an intimate relationship. If you have had a pattern of ending your relationships during this time, you can view previous short-term relationships as rehearsals. With each relationship, you learn something new about yourself and your choice of partners. It can take several partners, along with a fine-tuning process, before you settle down for the long term.

Heterosexuals go through the same process of short-term relationships. However, most heterosexuals have the advantage of going through their first relationships when they are in their teens. You may have missed out on these early experiences and had to wait until you were older. The other advantage heterosexuals have is that they talked incessantly during this time about their first sexual experiences, dating, and relationship experiences with their friends:

what they were doing well, and where they were making mistakes. Gay men often attempt their first relationships without having the built-in social support that high school brings.

As a result, your expectations of intimacy and relationships may need adjusting. You may not learn what to expect until after your first few relationships. For example, the Cinderella myth isn't exclusive to women; you may want to be rescued and taken care of. If so, you may need to find yourself in an unhealthy relationship or two before you realize that intimacy is based on equality.

After a few relationships, fine-tuning follows. Perhaps the earlier relationships didn't work out because the timing wasn't right. Or you didn't see the signs indicating that he wasn't ready for a relationship. Perhaps when it got serious, he ran away. Likewise, you may have found out some things about him that were unacceptable.

He was too . . .
Controlling;
Reclusive;
Needy.

He didn't . . .
Want enough sex;
Like my friends;
Care about me.

It could also be a fault of incompatibility. You . . .
Liked being around people and he didn't;
Argued all the time;
Wanted monogamy, but he didn't.

Another reason you may have not been able to get past this transitional time is that the risk of being hurt multiplies. Instead of facing your fears concerning the end of a relationship, you may have pushed your fears out of your awareness. Then, you used these other reasons as an excuse for an early exit.

You have two contradictory states of mind as you approach early intimacy: Desire and fear.

Your unconscious fear can outweigh your conscious desire to achieve intimacy; you may start putting up defenses and, in doing so, unwittingly sabotage your relationships. Here is an exercise to determine whether or not you have a greater amount of fear than desire:

★ EXERCISE: STOPPING THE REVOLVING DOOR

Below is a series of statements that will help you clarify how much fear of intimacy you possess. Answer the questions as honestly as you can. As a result, you may begin to be more cognizant about why you can't make the transition from dating to becoming committed boyfriends. With awareness, you have the ability to stop the revolving door. Rate the following items as Agree (A); Neutral (N); or Disagree (D).

1. *When break-ups happen, I jump back into dating right away.*
2. *I meet men who are from out of town or are in a relationship.*
3. *I mostly feel desperate.*
4. *I cry only when no one else is around.*
5. *I might be too picky.*

1. When break-ups happen, I jump back into dating right away.
Agreeing with this statement means that you may have a pattern of getting into rebound relationships. Not waiting until some time has passed before getting back in the saddle means you're looking for a

new partner to mitigate feelings of loss from your previous breakup. When a new boyfriend is merely an extension of your former partner or a way to distract you from grief, the new relationship doesn't have a good chance of lasting.

The amount of time it takes to heal from a long-term relationship varies. Some people take years to heal, others less time. It depends partly on how long you were together. But that's not all. You're losing the idea of a future with someone, which is why the amount of time you were together is only one factor.

Other factors include life circumstances, such as moving to a new city or experiencing the death of a friend or family member, which can lengthen the process. Conversely, you may have gone through a pre-grieving process (mourning the loss before it ends), which can shorten recovery time. You will know you have sufficiently recovered when you're able to replace your pain, anger, or bitterness with good memories and the knowledge that you have learned a valuable and constructive lesson. After some time has passed, be open to becoming friendly with your ex, or at least try not to avoid the places he frequents.

However, life often doesn't work according to the ideal. You might meet someone you're interested in before you have healed, and you may not want to lose the chance of forming a relationship with him. If this happens, you will have to make your new partner aware of your grief, and he should be sufficiently patient to help you through it. A relationship like this can work when the lines of communication stay wide open.

2. I meet men who are from out of town or who are in a relationship.

If you agreed with this statement, first note that random things sometimes happen. You meet someone at a party, and as you're handing him your card, he tells you he has only another few days in town before he heads home. Likewise, you might have asked yourself, "Why is it when I'm on vacation people flock to me, and not one person is interested in me here?" The important clue is to look for a trend. When it seems that all you find are unavailable people, it's bad news and good news.

The bad news is you may be letting fear overtake you; you may be fooling yourself into thinking that you are looking for a relationship but actually you are avoiding it. When you're out of town, you project openness and confidence because you feel you have nothing to lose, but this is not the same as risking intimacy. When you start a relationship with someone who lives in a different city, it can feel very intimate; but, in fact, it's a part-time relationship. You feel a strong emotional attachment partly because you wish you were living in closer proximity. However, the reality is that you don't have to commit at the same level as someone who lives in the same town or city.

The good news is that because we live in a global community, you may want to pursue a relationship with someone who lives in a different city. The key to discovering whether you are actually avoiding a relationship rather than moving toward one is to maintain an awareness of your motives. Do you have a pattern of pining to be in a relationship but finding excuses for why you're not?

The other good news is you could be in a trial-and-error phase of finding an intimate partner. You may be closer to being ready for intimacy and need time to figure out what *doesn't* work before you learn what does. In the meantime, you're learning different aspects of dating, communication, and intimacy.

3. I mostly feel desperate.

However easy it is for others to be aware of your desperation, you may be unable to see it for yourself. As a result, you must look for clues. One clue that you're desperate is when you tell your friends you're in a relationship, but when they ask how long you've been in it, you tell them it's been three weeks (or less!). Another clue is to extol the virtues of each potential partner, and either you were bitterly disappointed and ended it or they found ways to back off. A partner is not here to fulfill your needs. If you agreed with the third statement, take some time to get to know yourself, which means better self-care and learning why you feel desperate.

4. I cry only when no one else is around.

When you withhold your emotions in front of other people and release them when you are alone, you're going to have a hard time letting yourself become vulnerable. Sharing feelings is not limited to crying. When someone does something to upset you and you won't talk about your anger, pain, or disappointment, you will find it challenging to bring up difficult issues that arise during a long-term relationship. Start slowly in regard to airing your feelings. When someone hurts you, say "Ouch," or start out by saying, "I'm uncomfortable when you say that" rather than "I'm angry because you did this" or "I'm upset because you did that." Ease into sharing your more unpleasant emotions.

5. I might be too picky.

You don't want to have low standards, but be alert to the possibility that you have developed the "too-picky syndrome"; that is, finding fault with other men to the point where you don't date them or stop early on. It can be difficult to determine whether you have fallen into this trap. You may have to listen to your friends or go with your gut feelings. When you keep crossing guys off your list for different reasons, you have probably nit-picked your way out of a potential relationship. As often as not, agreeing with this statement means that your fear has provided you with an unconscious way to avoid intimacy.

If you have had a series of short-term relationships, you'll come to a point where you will feel the need to do the necessary work to stop repeating your patterns. When you feel blocked at the transitional phase, ask a third party to help you sort out your issues. It's never too early to start seeing a couples counselor. I wish all couples would consider counseling at the first signs of problems brewing. Many wait until it's too late: Pain, anger, and resentment have set in and too many damaging things have been said and done. When you see a counselor, you are still doing the work to make your relationship more intimate. You are simply asking a third party to help you change emerging patterns and give you guidance.

Part of the work is to become aware of your fears. *Of course* you're afraid. Everyone has some fear on board. As you acknowledge your fear and face it head on, you are already building the courage to trust, to be vulnerable, and to tolerate the uncertainty that occurs when you transition from dating to becoming partners.

Putting It Together

Early intimacy is a time that is filled with new experiences. If you become infatuated, it's fairly easy to lose perspective during this time. It's equally possible to sabotage your efforts as fears and insecurities rise to the surface. However, by staying in the driver's seat, keeping your perspective intact, and putting a stop to the revolving door, you can move smoothly toward a long-term relationship. Next, we turn to new challenges that arise when you transition to a more serious commitment.

CHAPTER 5

What to Expect as You Get Closer

AS YOU AND your partner move toward a more serious commitment, you encounter new experiences as you adjust to being together. At this stage, many couples move in together. Whether or not you start living together, however, you will face several changes. Adjusting to new challenges such as regaining independence, highlighting differences, and finding yourselves caught in power struggles tend to emerge during the first one or two years of being together.

Moving In

Moving in together is a step in commitment. Some couples wait as long as several years to combine households. The most common timeframe is anywhere from six months to a couple of years or more. I believe it's okay to be on the conservative side. When you decide to live together, you have two options. You can move into one of your existing places or look for a new place. Let's explore these options and consider ways to make a smooth transition.

Moving into an Existing Place

To start the discussion, consider Alex and Mark's situation.

CASE STUDY: *Alex and Mark*

It is three months into their relationship. Alex, who is thirty-four, is staying with Mark (thirty-six) six to seven nights a week. Alex's lease is coming up, and if he renews it he will have to have to sign for another year. Neither of them wants to wait that long. Mark's apartment has two bedrooms and is closer to where they both work, so Alex moves into Mark's place.

Because they are progressing quickly, Alex and Mark are going into a committed relationship while they're still in the honeymoon phase. They don't know each other very well, although they think they do, in part because they are relying on verbal assurances without verifying that their actions match the words. They are rapidly merging their two lives, but before they have gotten to know each other's faults and idiosyncrasies. A relationship like this can work, but it is challenging. One specific challenge is, as the following Red Flag brings up, How do you know you can trust him?

⚑ RED FLAG: *Trust Experience More than Words*

The biggest challenge of quickly moving in together comes from not knowing each other very well and a lack of shared experiences. Something could be really wrong with the other person that only time will reveal. If your partner says he uses drugs occasionally, how do you know whether he is minimizing or denying a drug problem? An initially charming individual can actually turn out to be very different from what he appears to be.

Excluding unusual circumstances, such as having an addiction or being abusive, you will typically face other challenges when you move in right away. For example, it may be too late before you learn that you have very different sets of friends or ways of approaching household chores. To think about what can happen when you take more time, contrast Alex and Mark's fast move-in experience with the following illustration.

CASE STUDY: *Jason and Gregory*

Jason bought the house that he mentioned he was looking at when they met online. Gregory continued to rent, keeping his own place.

After going out for about two years, they talk about moving in together. It makes sense to both of them that Gregory would move in with Jason. During their discussions, they decide that Gregory won't pay rent; rather, he will save the money and, after a few years, he will either pay Jason a lump sum that represents a percentage of ownership in the existing house or he will put his money toward the down payment on a house they will purchase together. They will each have a certain percentage of ownership in the new house and pay that percentage each month.

Because they waited two years, they are taking advantage of the many opportunities to talk about the logistics of moving in together and how their respective financial situations will affect the change. Jason knows it is up to him to help Gregory feel comfortable about moving into his home. As an important gesture, Jason offers to take some of his artwork down so that Gregory can put up some of his pieces. They replace some of Jason's furniture with Gregory's.

After two years of living together, Gregory is able to save enough money toward a down payment on a new house with 30 percent ownership. Although Jason has to put down more than Gregory, they are able to develop a plan they both feel comfortable with.

Sometimes, couples move into an existing place for economic or practical reasons. Although you're moving into his place, or vice versa, has its disadvantages, it can have the advantage of being less stressful. When you move into an existing place, at least one of you already knows where everything is (kitchen utensils, tools, supplies). You may choose to move things around, but that is less stressful than combining two households. Systems are in place (dressers, closets, drawers) and you add the new possessions to the existing systems. And you don't have to search for everyday objects.

If your partner moves into your place, talk about his concerns. Perhaps he has suggested to you, either directly or indirectly, that he is worried he won't have an area to call his own, won't be able to keep his belongings, or that he will be forced to leave. You can help reduce his fears. If you live in an apartment, ask the landlord to add him to the lease so that he obtains legal rights. If he can't be added to the lease, assume that he wants at least some of his furniture and household items in your place. Ask him where he thinks his favorite chair and desk should go. Make room for his car in the garage, if you have one. Don't assume you will use your dishes and silverware. Rather, ask which he prefers and begin the process of negotiation. The outcome should be that both of you will concede to the other person's wishes in some areas.

After he moves in, include him in decision making whenever possible. For example, when you're shopping for a new appliance, take him with you and welcome his suggestions. Give his preferences equal weight to yours. When he asks to contribute toward some of the cost, work together to decide what is fair. What about rent or mortgage and utilities? You have many options here: You might split the rent and utilities in half, arrange a proportional split, or decide that one partner will pay for everything. The decision will depend on your income levels and plans for the future. As with Jason and Gregory, you can be creative with your solution.

There's no right or wrong way to divide rent. Simply be aware of your motives for asking for what you want because it will have an affect on intimacy. For example, if your partner moves into your place and you insist that he not pay rent, is it because money isn't an issue or because you need to be in control? What will you do if your insistence causes him to feel embarrassed?

If you are thinking of moving into your partner's place, consider these issues but in reverse. How does he react to your suggestion that you move your couch and chair into his living room? How does he feel about putting up your artwork? Adding another phone line? Moving when you feel ready? His reactions and way of treating your wishes and concerns will signify what you can expect when you move in.

The "Business End" of Your Relationship

Your everyday life with your partner has an intimate part and a business part. The business aspect of your relationship includes decision making, household chores, and finances. The way you approach the business end of your relationship has a direct impact on the intimacy.

Regarding household chores, no two people have exactly the same requirements when it comes to neatness, cleanliness, and tolerance for things like dishes in the sink and dirty clothes. The further apart you are in relation to these issues, the more negotiating you will need to do before both of you feel comfortable.

If you make more money than your partner, first understand how you could abuse your power. To illustrate, some people might fall into the trap of reasoning that if they hire a house cleaner to come in every other week, their partners should, as a matter of course, clean on the off-weeks. However, it's only fair when you approach your partner to ask him whether he's comfortable with this arrangement. Furthermore, if he agrees to it, it should be understood that he has the right to let you know if it becomes a problem. Because you have more power than he does, he might downplay initial objections. He might feel bad for being unable to contribute toward a house cleaner. It's possible he will grow resentful over time, so opening the door to re-negotiating can help him address his feelings.

It's a tricky area, and I want to emphasize that the *way* you negotiate the business end of your relationship is more important than the *what*. Complaining, nagging, and threatening are short-term solutions that can have the effect of creating emotional distance. On the other hand, because you and your partner don't have the pre-determined areas of responsibility that exist for heterosexuals, you have the opportunity to design your relationship.

This gives you the chance to communicate your needs and talk more openly about what each of you expects and what each of you will do. As a result, you more freely negotiate your everyday life.

If you are like most people, how much money you make and how many assets you own are personal matters. When you have a partner, you are letting him into a private matter, which makes managing finances a part of intimacy. Many couples run aground about issues related to money, and the subject is often cited as a reason for severe problems. Partners often expect that when they get together, they're going to combine their money and assets. Although some couples don't wait very long, others wait for years before combining, and some never do. What are your expectations about finances, and how have your expectations affected your relationship? If your expectations don't match, how close are they, and how do you handle your differences diplomatically?

Moving to a New Place

When you and your partner move into a new place, you have the advantage of starting off with a feeling of equality. It feels more like "our place" rather than his place or your place. The space is new to both of you, so there's less chance to become territorial.

Although this feeling of equality is a great advantage, moving to a new place is more stressful than moving into an existing one. Part of the stress of moving to a new place involves doubling the amount of packing, moving, storing, and everything else it takes to combine two households. Then you have to blend your tastes, styles, and preferences into a space neither of you has had previous experience with.

However, many of the same considerations as moving into an existing residence need to be taken into account. For instance, if you are the partner with the greater income, be aware that sharing decision making can prevent future problems. No matter which decisions you make, talk it over, sleep on it, and then talk some more. This process should continue until both of you are comfortable with your decisions. When you have ongoing talks about moving in, you are giving yourselves time to think about these issues and take creative approaches.

Deciding Not to Move In

Certain life circumstances—for example, each of you owns a home—might cause you to decide to move forward and become committed without moving in together. You may have grown used to having your own place and don't want to move in at all. As long as the other person feels the same way, you are still on your way to an intimate, satisfying relationship. Even though I won't go into detail about Roberto and David's situation just yet, that's exactly what our third couple decides to do. They haven't closed themselves off to the possibility that they might move in together at some time, but they don't see it for the foreseeable future.

If you choose not to move in together, you could face decisions about who is going to stay at whose place. You might stay at his place most of the time, he might stay at yours, or maybe you will split the difference. This arrangement works well for many couples, even long-term. In a sense, you'd each have a second home.

Challenges in a New Relationship

Whether you have moved in together or not, let's say that your new relationship is proceeding along fine, and you have dealt with the challenges noted in the last chapter. Then, out of nowhere, a blindsiding bump in the road appears. You feel a jolt. As it often happens, the honeymoon phase ends around the time you move in together. When infatuation fades, you experience a sense of disillusionment. As a result, the end of the honeymoon is a difficult time. Even if you didn't have a honeymoon period, several threats to the relationship may appear. With little time to establish a shared history, to get to know each other on a deeper level, and to acquire mutual friends, you and your partner are afraid because you perceive the emerging challenges as a threat. New threats include:

- *Falling off the pedestal*
- *Highlighting differences*
- *Navigating power struggles*
- *Reconsidering sex*
- *Regaining independence*
- *Coping with periods of emotional distance*

Let's look at how each of these threats impacts intimacy, as well as ways to minimize their impact.

Falling off the Pedestal

When you first got together with your partner, you thought he was wonderful partly because you didn't know much about him except the way he was treating you. Because you wanted the relationship to go forward, you placed positive attributes onto why he was treating you that way. He seemed nothing but sweet, delightful, and amazing.

Over time, you may find yourself feeling let down. As you become disillusioned, you will begin to fill in new blanks as to what causes him to behave in certain ways. Quite often, this leads to emotional distance. For example, imagine you've become monogamous and have developed the unrealistic expectation that neither of you will be attracted to other people because he was once entirely focused on you. When he looks at another guy, you feel let down.

Alternatively, the characteristics that you initially found attractive transform into the very traits that you later find frustrating or off-putting. For example, let's say you tend to be an anxious and over-achieving person, and you were initially attracted to someone whom you perceived to be laid back and cool under pressure. After some times passes, the idea that he's laid back turns into thinking that he's lazy, detached or uncaring.

When you regarded him as the most wonderful guy in the world, his standing had nowhere to go but down. As he lets you down, you have the opportunity to acquire a more realistic picture of him. Regardless of when you moved in or when the honeymoon ended, it's a good idea to ask yourself whether you are willing to do what it takes to build genuine intimacy with this person. To establish a genuine connection, idealistic notions about your partner have to come to an end.

Another kind of idealization that needs to be looked at is when you unconsciously reveal information about who you want to be (your ideal self) rather than who you really are (your real self). This is revealed when you make "I am" statements. Such statements can reveal what you wish was true. I'm not suggesting that most people lie about themselves, but people unconsciously reveal their ideal selves when they use these statements.

For example, let's say you repeatedly insist that you are "completely honest" whenever your new boyfriend suspects that you're not telling the truth. You are describing an ideal rather than the real you because no one is honest all the time. Do you avoid telling the truth because you don't want to hurt other people? Because you want to get out of uncomfortable situations? Think about the times you stretch the truth, omit certain information, and outright cover up. Just as it's helpful for intimacy to reduce idealization of a new partner, it's good to try to close the gap between your real self and your ideal self. You come into the relationship with less defensiveness and more authenticity.

Highlighting Differences

As you idealized your partner, you spent a lot of time and energy identifying what the two of you have in common. It was natural for you not to want to look at your differences because you feared it might create a problem. This fear could have caused you to dismiss differences of opinion, interests, and wants and needs.

||||||||||||||||||||||||||||||||||||||||||||||||||||||||||||||||||||||||||||||||||||||||||||||||||||||||||||||||||

When differences arise, try not to view them as threats to intimacy. Instead, learn to appreciate your differences.

||||||||||||||||||||||||||||||||||||||||||||||||||||||||||||||||||||||||||||||||||||||||||||||||||||||||||||||||||

Almost imperceptibly, a shift occurs until, one day, you can't seem to take the focus away from how different the two of you are. You concentrate on areas where you are poles apart. To sort out this issue, think of your differences as ends of a spectrum; for example, from frugal to spender, from spontaneous to planner, or from shy to outgoing. In addition, here are a few more opposites:

- *Optimistic/Pessimistic*
- *Neat/Messy*
- *Thoughtful/Inconsiderate*
- *Pragmatic/Idealistic*
- *Laid-Back/High Maintenance*
- *Domineering/Passive*

Note that not all differences between partners are going to be exact opposites. To illustrate, a person can be fairly submissive under many circumstances but not all the time. Someone can be mostly shy but more outgoing when he gets to know people.

There are as many *reasons* for differences between partners as there are differences. Every person is raised within an ethnic culture(s), and most people are brought up in households that practice some form of organized religion. Along with ethnic and religious differences, people raised in the city can be very different from those raised in the country.

Beyond these, each person is raised in a unique family culture. It's quite possible that two people who were raised in a large city, are the same age, and have parents who are ethnically and religiously the same can be very different because one person had strict caregivers, the other permissive ones; or one person had no siblings, the other several brothers and sisters.

Each family has what I call "family mottoes." These are ways of acting, believing, and thinking specific to your family of origin but are presented as and believed to be universal truths. Add those differences to how we learn to perceive our worlds as children (much of which we carry to adulthood), and you have the basis for each person's unique set of attitudes, beliefs, and behaviors.

Regarding these differences, try to fight the tendency to want him to be more like you. Recognize that the shift from focusing on similarities to acknowledging differences is inevitable. View some of your differences as complementary rather than antagonistic. Synergistically, each of your strengths becomes a relationship strength. When one of you has a particular skill, these previously individual abilities now belong to the relationship.

For example, if you enjoy gardening but your partner doesn't, your relationship now has a gardener. If your partner is great at finances, your relationship has gained a bookkeeper. The same goes for shopping, decorating, and other household responsibilities. It is inevitable, however, that you will both dislike certain duties, so divide them up between you or alternate times for performing them.

Learning to accept some differences is related to letting go. When he does something you don't approve of and it's not directly affecting you, ask yourself why you want him to be different. You may be operating out of the unconscious belief that your "other half" somehow belongs to you or is a reflection of you, or perhaps you expect him to behave according to your family mottoes. This forces you to make a conscious effort to let go of trying to change him.

In which areas should you let go of trying to change him? To begin with, any area that he says you're intruding into. For example, do you think that your partner should behave differently in public or among friends? If he asks your opinion about this, feel free to tell him.

However, is this something you argue about? If so, you might feel embarrassed about one of his qualities; therefore, you want him to be different *for you*. You're not acting in his best interest and instead see him as your reflection.

As another example: Let's say you don't like certain clothes your partner wears. When you tell him to get rid of his old clothes, criticize him, or try to convince him he needs new ones, he can easily become defensive. If he resists, arguments will ensue and possibly lead to emotional distance. The following exercise is designed to help you examine your differences.

★ EXERCISE: EXAMINING YOUR DIFFERENCES

Take a moment to write down the differences between you and your partner. The list can include ethnicity, politics, spirituality, family of origin, personality, ongoing activities, and outlook, among others. Political and spiritual differences are self-explanatory. Family of origin differences include your family's socioeconomic status, education, birth order, and degree of family dysfunction (alcoholism, abuse, etc.). Ongoing activity differences are behaviors such as going to bars, how you like to spend your relaxation time (reading, watching television), and amount of alone time you need. Outlook differences include your picture of an ideal partner, expectation of monogamy, and long-term plans for the future.

The key to working through your differences is to respect the way your partner handles his life. This will have the largest impact on how you handle conflict. When two people are in a relationship, conflicts arise out of differences, and each couple decides (not always consciously) how much they are going to acknowledge and deal with conflict; this, in turn, influences intimacy. More important than the type of differences you have is the amount of respect you have for your differences. If you want him to be like you and you're trying to change him, you will engage in power struggles.

||||||||||||||||||||||||||||||||||||||||||||||||||||||||||||||||||||||||||||||||||||||||||||||||||||||||||||||||||||||||

Spirituality

When you and your partner have similar spiritual beliefs, intimacy increases when you share in spiritual rituals and find ways to express your spirituality together. Let's say, however, you're with someone whose spiritual beliefs are different from yours. You are still able to share in certain rituals.

It's less complicated when your differences aren't very far apart. Let's say you both have a religion: You're both Christian, and if you are Lutheran and your partner is Presbyterian, you may find it easier to find a common place of worship than, say, if you are Pentecostal and your partner is Jewish. With creative thinking, you will find new ways to reconcile your differences. To think about your own solutions, consider Roberto and David's situation.

CASE STUDY: *Roberto and David*

Roberto was raised Catholic. After becoming an adult, he spent several years shunning any form of religion. He had never lost his belief in God, but he is unhappy with the church's stance on homosexuality. Roberto spent years "shopping" for a new spiritual home, trying several denominations. None was satisfying to him because he wasn't familiar with their ways of worshipping.

One day, Roberto goes to a gay-affirming Catholic church. He is happy to have found many of the same rituals and songs of his youth. He finds it comforting. He is excited about it, and he asks David to go to services with him. David, who is Jewish, accompanies him to services, but after a few months, he tells Roberto he isn't comfortable going. Roberto is upset, but at the same time he understands.

Before living with Roberto, David had been going to services on Friday nights since he was in his early twenties. After they got together, David barely managed to make it to temple once a month. As Roberto was searching for a new church home, David realized he was missing the services and the community feeling. So David started attending regularly. Now that David and Roberto are attending separate services, Roberto is concerned that too much time is being spent separately.

After some time passes, Roberto and David come up with a solution. Ordinarily, David goes to temple on Saturday mornings. But, once a month, David brings Roberto to Friday-night services, and they go to dinner with a few people that David knows from the temple. Also once a month Roberto brings David to the MCC church instead of the Catholic church because David feels more comfortable there. Even though Roberto and David's spiritual beliefs are different, they are finding a way for common spiritual expression, which in turn enhances closeness.

> Your differences don't have to interfere with intimacy. More important than sharing similar beliefs is how you handle your differences. If you belittle your partner's beliefs, or try to have him believe the way you do, you will run into major points of contention. Treat his views as seriously as you do your own. When you support your partner's spiritual beliefs, you are maintaining, and even enhancing, closeness with your partner.

Navigating Power Struggles

When you and your partner call attention to your differences, power struggles often follow. Power struggles have an underlying theme, namely, "whose way are we going to do things?" Because there's a right/wrong belief (I'm right/he's wrong), they may not appear to each partner as such. A sense of self-righteousness, coupled with a sense of importance in the moment, is what makes power struggles so challenging. One clue that you're having power struggles is when disagreements take on a sense of urgency that is out of proportion to what's going on. Here's a list of many ways that partners try to struggle for control.

1. Leaving Notes

It's one thing to leave a quick note or to text your partner when you forget something. But e-mailing, texting, or leaving notes to communicate how you feel about something he did or to bring up an issue leads to a loss of intimacy. Furthermore, unless you've tried them and you already know that they don't cause emotional distance, avoid e-mail fights.

When you leave notes about important issues, are you afraid to talk about the subject or bring it up? Are you concerned how he will react? Do you not want to rock the boat? Your boat is already rocking, so it's better to talk about it. An exception is when you're afraid you'd get too angry or he consistently becomes defensive and cuts you off when you want to broach a subject. In that case, you may have little choice.

2. Bickering

Every couple disagrees at times. But bickering is a form of jockeying for control. There's a winner and a loser, and because neither partner wants to lose, the arguments deteriorate into squabbling. Alex and Mark, who went from honeymooning to not getting along, spend much of their time bickering.

CASE STUDY: *Alex and Mark*

Whenever Mark is driving, Alex complains that Mark is driving too fast, not looking out for pedestrians, and not using the turn signal. The following argument typifies their interaction: After Alex complains a few times, Mark says, "I have never gotten into an accident, unlike you." Alex replies, "It doesn't matter. One of these days you're going to get us into an accident, and I don't feel safe." Mark: "But your constant commenting on my driving is making me nervous, so I'm a worse driver when you're in the car." Alex: "But your driving makes me anxious. When I say something, I feel better, so get used to it." Mark: "Fine, then you drive us everywhere we go"; and, of course, that would never happen. The next time Mark drives, it's a variation on the same theme. Each time it leaves them feeling annoyed and frustrated.

3. Assuming Your Partner Is a Mind Reader

Let's say you're being distant with your partner, and he asks what he's done to upset you. You don't reveal what you're thinking; instead, you tell him that he should already know why. He gives it some thought but can't come up with an answer. You go silent after a deep sigh.

When you are upset with your partner and he doesn't know the reason, resist the temptation to think he knows why you're mad at him. Although you believe he *should* know what you're thinking, he isn't wrong for not knowing. When he never gets an answer, the two of you will not resolve the issue. Eventually, he will start to walk on eggshells because he's wondering whether what he's saying or doing is going to upset you.

To avoid this, don't expect your partner to know what you're thinking or feeling. Assume your partner *doesn't* know, and answer him directly when he asks what's wrong. Better yet, let him know before he asks, which is taking responsibility for the way you feel. This opens the possibility for you to work through the problem together.

4. Not Picking Your Battles

Making everything into an issue inhibits intimacy. So, pick your battles. Perhaps the best way to think about picking your battles is this: What are some unusual traits of yours that he has to live with? If you know he has an especially hard-wired trait, what's the point of bringing it up when you know it will only start an argument?

When you ask your partner to do something, and he does it, refrain from criticizing him. Let's say you ask him to mop the floor. The first time he does it, thank him and praise him, even if all he did was smear dirt around because he didn't change the water in the bucket. Don't clean up after him, and avoid criticizing him. After the fourth or fifth mopping, thank him as usual but ask for permission to add a suggestion. If he says yes (which he probably will, because now he knows you won't simply criticize him), suggest he change the water occasionally because then the floor will be even cleaner.

You may react negatively to my suggestion that you praise your partner because you think praising him is manipulative or would be treating him like a dog. However, consider this: Partners punish each other through criticism, anger, periods of silence, getting back, and so on. So why not use praise? Praise reinforces good behavior, whereas punishing him teaches him to avoid punishment, sometimes to the point of avoiding the punisher.

5. Using Hot-Button Words

Hot-button words are expressions you already know will start a fight. Let's say that telling your partner to calm down just upsets him more. Then, you're "off to the races." Over time, the pattern becomes so predictable that it's like a script: You can guess the outcome before you start. If you know your partner reacts negatively to certain words or phrases, state them differently or avoid them altogether. And if you can accurately predict that your partner will respond defensively or angrily, it's time to start asking yourself why you do it. I go more in depth into this "why" question in chapter 7.

6. Getting into the Round-and-Round

The round-and-round goes something like this: "You said you were going to pick Buddy up at the dog groomer." *"No I didn't."* "Yes you did. At breakfast you said you were going to the gym and then you were going to get him." *"What I said was I was going to go to the gym, so could you pick up Buddy?"* "You did not. If you asked me, I would have told you I was going to lunch with Roger and I wouldn't have time to pick him up." Meanwhile, poor Buddy sits at the groomer while you argue over who said what.

Arguing about what was said in the past leads to the round-and-round. Talk about what you *intended* to say, and then he can say what he intended to say. Better yet, tell him what you want to communicate now, and then you can go from there. Accept what your partner says, and ask him to do the same so that you don't argue about what was said earlier.

A variation of the round-and-round is the hot potato of blame. In the hot potato, a situation occurs and each wants to blame the other. An "it's your fault" argument ensues. One way around the hot-potato is to focus on *the situation* rather than each other when something goes wrong. For example, if you're both running late for something, express your annoyance at being late rather laying the blame at your partner's doorstep. As another example, if a bill went unpaid, focus on paying it and finding a solution for future payments rather than arguing about who forgot. In general, avoid the round-and-round to make your disagreements more productive and to steer clear of the emotional distance it can bring.

7. The See-Saw Syndrome

Remember when you were a kid and you'd get on the see-saw in the playground? When you were up on the see-saw, the other person was down. It is not unusual to enter a pattern in which both partners can't seem to feel good about the relationship, feel close, or behave pleasantly at the same time. The see-saw comes from a variety of reasons, including competition or an unconscious need to be on top. When you're on the see-saw, level it out by starting a dialogue about your observation of this phenomenon.

8. The "I Dunno" Trap

You and your partner can find yourselves in a pattern, or more of a rut, when your partner says, "Where would you like to go for dinner tonight?" You say, "I dunno, where do you want to go?" If you don't offer suggestions or if you look too sheepish, your partner may get frustrated.

Here's a variation, known as the bait-and-switch. He asks you where you want to go. You say "I dunno." *"How about if we go to Farfalla's for Italian food?"* "Nah, I don't want Italian food." *"How about Rambuttan for Thai food?"* "I don't like Rambuttan." He asks you about four more places to go, and you say no to all of them—but you still don't have an opinion.

If you do this, make a resolution to answer his question to the best of your ability. When you can't think of a place to go, suggest a type of food you feel in the mood for. Or tell him you'd rather eat in. But offer an idea, even if you don't care where you go. You will be saving him from becoming increasingly frustrated with your indecision.

9. The Chameleon Effect

Acting like a chameleon is an attempt to adapt to every situation, to be accepted and liked by everyone, and to please others at all costs. You may have feelings of inadequacy and try to overcome them by gaining universal acceptance or attempting to fit in with various groups of people.

On the plus side, a small amount makes you more flexible. However, you may have too fluid of an identity. The chameleon has no solid boundaries, preferences, likes and dislikes, opinions, or feelings. Your partner may become frustrated; he may start to lose respect for someone who always blends in. The chameleon may also have an intense need to avoid conflict, and what can start out looking like relationship harmony can turn into a feeling of living with a "yes man." Consider ways, such as reading, therapy, and other forms of personal growth to develop your identity, and let your partner know you are working on it. If you're living with a chameleon, put your frustration aside when you talk to him. Approach him in a caring way and ask him whether he knows why he does this. Let him know how this affects you.

10. Avoiding Conflict

Every couple has conflicts. The difference is whether or not you acknowledge and deal with them in a constructive way. Should you and your partner avoid conflict, your relationship will develop a polite quality. Both of you will harbor private grievances and resentments; one day, you will grow apart or one of you will find your anger and resentment building up to an explosion. When the tendency to avoid conflict lasts, it may even be "easier" to end the relationship than to deal with what's going on.

To learn to engage in productive conflict, test the waters by bringing up a small issue. For example, start with something like asking him to say hello and give you a kiss when he comes home. You may be paving the way for him to clear the air about issues he wants to bring up. Remember, the issues are already there. By discussing them, the only difference is that you're acknowledging them.

11. Cashing In

When you cash in, you go back several weeks, months, or even years to bring up past infractions and then lay them out all at once. Cashing in usually happens during an argument, when each of you is trying to prove a point. For example, to show your partner that he doesn't care about you, you list every uncaring action since the beginning of the relationship, such as the time he forgot your birthday or didn't notice your new haircut, or the day you specifically asked him for something he refused to do.

Rather than cashing in, air one or two issues at a time. Incorporate this into picking your battles. At the least, ask yourself why you wait until you are boiling mad to tell him what's going on with you, and why you feel compelled to go back and list every wrongdoing.

12. Needing to Have the Last Word

In an argument, do you need to have the last word? If so, consider what it's about. Usually, it is related to having to be right. You may also be avoiding a certain feeling, which may be shame or false pride. The next time you have an argument, let your partner have the last word and see what feelings come up. At the same time, remember that there's no right or wrong when it comes to arguing. It's a matter of having two points of view. If your partner needs to have the last word, you can let him, but you have the right to talk about it. As to the timing? Bring it up when he's not doing it.

13. Getting into Theoretical Arguments

You and your partner may get into an argument based on an incident or problem that could happen in the future. These arguments usually start with "What if you ..." or "What if I ..." statements. For instance, you say to your partner, "What would you do if I told you that this guy hit on me at work?"

Try to figure out why you would want to have a discussion based on something that hasn't happened. Perhaps you're telling your partner something but you think he will have trouble handling it. Perhaps you're trying to test the strength of your relationship or his level of commitment. As with countering some of the other power struggles, be direct. Even though it carries more risk, ask him about the relationship and talk about your fears.

14. Attack-Defend Communication

Attack-defend communication is an accusation followed by a defensive response. The attack may start out with these words: "Why did you do such-and-such?" For example, "You said you were going to pick up dinner. Why did you forget?" A more indirect attack is "I don't know why you'd conveniently forget to pick up dinner." Your partner will most likely feel the need to defend himself and explain why he failed to do it. Another type of attack starts with "Don't you think ... ?" (as in "Don't you think you're being childish?").

In the attack-defend style of communicating, the attacker is having feelings he's not bringing up and the defender feels angry about having to justify himself. So, instead of "Why did you forget to pick dinner up?" try, for example, "I'm annoyed that you didn't pick up dinner."

Replace "Don't you think you're being childish?" with "It upsets me when you pout."

Likewise, you don't have to defend yourself when you partner attacks you. Instead, take the following two-pronged approach. First, you don't have to answer a question just because it was asked. "Why did you forget to call me?" can be answered with "You sound angry I forgot." You're addressing the problem he is bringing up without getting defensive. Second, bring up the issue of how his attacks affect you—but do it later. Let him know that you would prefer that he state his problems directly by mentioning what you did and how it caused him to feel.

Avoiding Power Struggles

As you have seen, there are many variations on the theme of power struggles and ways to overcome them. Overall, if you are aware that your differences are threatening, and that control issues have led to these struggles, you can move beyond the struggle for power if you employ communication and patience. As Jason and Gregory's situation illustrates, however, you can also try to circumvent them.

CASE STUDY: *Jason and Gregory*

Because Jason and Gregory dated for a couple of years before living together, Jason knew that Gregory was a homebody and didn't like to socialize much with others. But he didn't realize it was going to bother him until they were living together. So, after Gregory moved in, Jason resolved that Gregory's lack of interest in going out was not going to deter him from having a good social life. However, instead of pressuring Gregory to go out with him and his friends, Jason usually invites him and accepts no for an answer. As a way to consider Gregory's feelings, Jason limits himself to going out with friends every couple of weeks, reminds Gregory he can come with him any time he wants to, and gives him at least a week's notice.

Jason accommodates Gregory by going out with friends less often than when they first met. Going out with friends is very important to Jason, and his relationship would have been more of a struggle if he had attempted to change Gregory, who is perfectly content to stay home while Jason goes out. He also realizes that no matter how much Gregory comes close to his ideal, they would still have their differences.

Reconsidering Sex

Some couples never reduce how often they have sex. They start out with once or twice a week (or once a day) and keep the pace. However, changes usually include having sex less often that's less hot. Let's say that before the relationship you were getting your sexual needs met by having anonymous sex. For the first few months of the new relationship, sex with your new boyfriend was great partly because of the newness. But the novelty wears off and the shift is a major adjustment.

In addition to natural shifts, a change in your sex life can stem from feeling distant and angry or having unresolved issues. Let's say you harbor resentment about something he did to you. If you're like most people, you find it difficult to have sex with your partner when you're angry with him. Underlying issues need to be addressed if you are to resume an enjoyable sex life.

Some couples never had great sex to begin with, and they wonder whether they made the right choice in a partner. Others first consider the type of person to whom they are emotionally attracted. For these men, a relationship can work if they focus on the emotional component. Likewise, some men do not need to be physically attracted to their partners to have sex with them; instead, they focus on other attributes. Just like other differences, sexual variations are neither right nor wrong. They are simply different ways of approaching sex. You ultimately have to decide what is right for you.

If both of you are monogamous, you won't need to negotiate having sex outside the relationship. But let's say your partner decides he no longer wants to be exclusive. You can't "make" him monogamous, but you still have room for negotiation. (I discuss this issue in chapter 10.)

You and your partner probably have different sex drives. For example, your partner may want to have sex once a week or so, but you want it more often. You may also have differences in the kinds of sex you prefer, in the time of day you enjoy it the most, and in your various fantasies. Most differences can be accommodated, such as encouraging masturbation for the person with the higher libido. Communication is key: An open and nonjudgmental attitude is important to working out your differences.

You might have mistakenly thought that once you were in a relationship, attraction to others would stop. It may for a while, but it's natural to have future attractions, crushes, and fantasies. Being in a relationship doesn't change this. However, you are in control of what you do about them. If you choose monogamy, then you will have to be careful not to put yourself in risky situations. Saying "I'd never . . . " is a reflection of inexperience. Saying "I need to stay away from . . . " is more realistic.

Over time, sex can take on a new meaning with your partner; when this happens, sex can be more satisfying because it communicates your feelings toward him. You want to please him because you enjoy doing so, and you communicate love and caring for him. In other words, sex becomes more emotionally based.

Regaining Independence

Imagine that you and your partner are standing a few feet apart and looking at each other. Then, imagine that each of you slowly turns outward. You periodically turn toward each other, sometimes at the same time, and other times one of you looks at the other person, who is looking in a different direction.

This picture represents the transition for most relationships. Initially, you were both focused on each other. As you settle in for the long term, you look at the world *and* at each other. Sometimes you focus on each other with equal intensity. At other times, one person is more into the other. The initial turning toward away is the process of regaining independence. You rekindle old friendships, take up a former hobby, start back to the gym, and return to activities you had given up. The interests that went away are coming back into focus, which can be threatening to the relationship because the need for independence can be misconstrued as a loss of love or desire. Think about how you would handle friendships, as Alex and Mark's situation illustrates.

CASE STUDY: *Alex and Mark*

Recall that Alex and Mark moved in together after knowing each other for three months. During the first year of living together, Alex neglected his friends, and his friend Sherly was particularly upset because they never saw each other. One day, Alex informs Mark he wants to have dinner with Sherly by himself. Mark says it is fine, and Alex and Sherly meet for dinner.

The next day, Mark is cold. Alex asks Mark what's wrong, but Mark says everything is fine. In a few days, life is back to normal. A few weeks later, Alex tells Mark he made plans to see some friends during the week, on a night he thought Mark would be working late. Mark gets angry and tells Alex he isn't working that night and that he should have been consulted first. Mark then runs into the bedroom and slams the door. After a few moments, Alex can't stand it and he follows Mark into the bedroom. Mark is lying on the bed, face down, and Alex tells Mark he will cancel his plans. Mark admits he is being childish and sheepishly tells Alex to go ahead. He doesn't sound too convincing, so Alex breaks his plans.

A pattern is beginning to emerge. When Alex wants to be with his friends, Mark says okay but then withdraws. Alex, who is worried about how Mark feels, tries to smooth things over because he doesn't want to hurt him.

When you reassure your partner that you still care for him and want to be together, you open up a discussion of your feelings regarding the shift to regained independence. In fact, you don't have to act out your feelings, as Alex and Mark do. Instead, talk them out.

Coping with Periods of Emotional Distance

As the desire for independence emerges, you may begin to feel uncomfortable. You might feel rejected, thinking he doesn't care about you as much as he used to. You might think that he'd rather be _____ (insert a phrase here: with his friends, on the Internet) than with you. You're upset most likely because you are interpreting his desire for time away from you as a threat to the relationship. But emotional distance is a natural consequence of being in a relationship.

You will most likely feel anxious or uncomfortable when your partner wants to reclaim his space. The feelings can become so uncomfortable that you will need reassurance from him that your relationship is okay. It is natural for you to want reassurance, but it may be hard to ask for it directly because it puts you in a vulnerable position. However, instead of allowing yourself to show your vulnerability, you might start an argument. Ironically, there is an intense connection during the altercation and, as important, a renewed sense of closeness when you make up. This can lead to further attempts to get your reassurance needs met through a cycle of fighting and making up.

If you're picking a fight to gain reassurance, think about asking directly for what you need.

Rather than getting caught up in this pattern, gather the courage to tell him how you're feeling. Learn to tolerate periods of distance as natural fluctuations. Ask him for reassurance when you need it, and offer him the same.

Putting It Together

The first couple of years together typically prove to be a time of adjustment. Though many couples move in during this time, some choose to live separately. Either way, the adjustment includes an attempt by each partner to regain a sense of independence, often highlighting new challenges that result in emphasizing differences and creating power struggles. Now that we have considered some general ways to deal with this uneasy period, let's look into specific tools that you can use to deepen intimacy as you continue to get a handle on these emerging issues.

CHAPTER 6

Building the Foundation for Deeper Intimacy

WE'VE SEEN SOME of the challenges you can expect as you adjust to a new relationship. Because this is a period of adjustment, it's important to consider techniques that will help give you the awareness, flexibility, self-confidence, and resources to take your relationship to a deeper level of intimacy. You may find the transition smoother if you examine your beliefs about what a relationship should look like.

Building Intimacy by Investigating Your Outlook

Throughout the first several chapters, we considered intimacy as an individual process, such as knowing yourself and considering your values, as well as a mutual process that includes reciprocal self-disclosure and trust. In this chapter, we consider tools that have elements of both, with an emphasis on how adjusting your outlook affects the mutual process of taking intimacy to a deeper level. These tools provide you with ways to:

- *Change your expectations*
- *Let go of trying to control your partner*
- *See beyond right and wrong*
- *Look at your differences in a positive way*
- *Cooperate and share power*

Change Your Expectations

Let's see how you can adjust certain expectations. In the first several months, you probably spent a lot of time with each other. Expect the amount of time you spend together to decrease. Note that some couples enjoy working and living together, but they are rare, and all the more power to them. However, most of us reach a comfort level with how much time we want to spend with our partners, with friends and family, and by ourselves.

As much as you may still want to spend every minute with your partner, consider occasionally spending an afternoon or evening apart. You could go out with friends or join a social or political group. When you have a night out with friends, sometimes you may want to bring your partner; at other times you'll want to go by yourself. Either way, keep up with at least part of your former routine while you continue to make room for him in your life.

You also need to adjust the expectation you will get along 100 percent of the time. As your differences emerge, you'll have disagreements. You should be able to disagree with your partner yet still respect his position. Also, expect to argue. Arguments are more intense than disagreements. Expect them to occur with varying frequency throughout your relationship. Arguments are also a natural part of having differences, and when you argue at least occasionally, you are enhancing intimacy by not sweeping issues under the rug.

High or unrealistic expectations can be harmful. If you go into a relationship with your eyes open to the reality he is a fallible human being—a person who has his good points and bad, strengths and weaknesses, and areas of insecurity—you have a much better chance of building intimacy.

Let Go of Trying to Control Your Partner

Refusing to accept your differences or resisting your partner's wishes to have more independence can give rise to the need to control him.

Unfortunately, attempting to control your partner creates conflict and tension.

Let's first distinguish between being controlling and being in control of your own life. The latter is, in fact, helpful to your relationship. When you feel you're in control of your own life, you have a job you feel good about (or are able to leave if you don't), you maintain good friendships, and you live in a place you're comfortable with. A person who exhibits self-control has little need to control others. He sees the world as a fairly safe place, acts independently, believes that other people have the right to the same degree of independence, and takes responsibility for his decisions.

Controlling behavior, on the other hand, comes from the opposite feeling. A controlling person tries to soothe the anxiety that arises as a result of feeling threatened. Threats can be anything from a change in routine to feelings of intense jealousy. A person who needs to control his environment (which includes other people) doesn't know he's doing this until he involves himself in a process of self-discovery.

A controlling person needs to have power over others because there are areas in his life in which he feels unhappy or that are unmanageable. He may be insecure (or jealous) and believe he must control his partner to prevent him from leaving. Sometimes, the need to dominate others began in childhood as a result of growing up in a dysfunctional family: Chaos was the norm and there was no sense of personal control. This trait is unconscious, so the following exercise can help you determine whether you're controlling.

★ EXERCISE: ARE YOU CONTROLLING?

To figure this out, you need to look for clues. One place to look is your behavior. When you're feeling insecure, do you check up on your partner or read his e-mail? Do you try to stop him from seeing certain friends? Do you yell, threaten, or ask a lot of questions? When you're feeling unhappy, do you take it out on him because he's closest to you? Tell your partner he needs to change? Complain? In general, do you think that if only he had enough information, he'd see things your way? Get mad when he doesn't do what you tell him to do?

If you are a controlling person, it should not come as a surprise when the day comes that your partner will be dissatisfied. As he becomes dissatisfied, he may go back to school, find a better job, or figure out other ways to prepare himself to gain more self-control. He may also reach the tipping point of beginning to question the relationship.

Think about how you can stop controlling your partner. Exploring this topic takes a third party, usually a therapist, to help you because there is a tornado of feelings inside of you, including insecurity, neediness, and fear of abandonment. You most likely need help in figuring out what's going on and why. A detailed discussion of the ways to deal with your feelings goes beyond the scope of this book, but I touched on the subject to help you become aware of it.

See Beyond Right and Wrong

To sustain intimacy, go beyond the notion of right and wrong. I'm not talking about being right and wrong in a moral sense. Rather, as you settle into living together, you can develop struggles over who's right concerning points of view, ways you remember past experiences, and your respective approaches to doing things. As you think about this, consider Jason and Gregory's situation.

CASE STUDY: *Jason and Gregory*

Gregory is sympathetic to Jason's recovery, but he also wants to have a good time occasionally. Though Jason is on sure footing about staying sober, he stays away from clubs and doesn't want alcohol kept in the house. Gregory agreed to this, even though throughout his adult life he had always had a few bottles of wine on hand. Nonetheless, when they go out to dinner, Gregory feels comfortable about having a drink or a glass of wine in front of Jason. The only time Gregory drinks a bit more is when he goes out with his friends. Jason doesn't mind Gregory's coming home slightly buzzed, but he asked Gregory to not talk about how much he drinks or about drinking in general. Gregory agreed, and this arrangement works well for them. Once in a while, Gregory comments about a bit of guilt he's feeling, and Jason reassures him that abstaining from alcohol is something he chooses and that Gregory's drinking doesn't tempt him.

One day, Gregory and Jason decide to throw a holiday party. They agree that they can't have a party without alcohol available for guests. Jason says he isn't worried about having alcohol in the house as long as it's taken out after the party. Gregory says he will ask one of his friends to take home any remaining alcohol. On the night of their party, Gregory doesn't drink as a silent gesture of support.

You can see from their interaction that Jason and Gregory are aware of each other's sensitive areas and agree that each of them should live their social lives according to how they feel they should. They gain more from their compromises than they lose. Let's compare the way Jason and Gregory worked out their situation to Alex and Mark's emerging power struggle.

CASE STUDY: *Alex and Mark*

Alex and Mark are having an ongoing struggle around friendships. Alex occasionally won't tell Mark where he's going and who he's going out with. A more serious problem starts when Alex starts hanging out with his ex, Paul. Alex and Paul were together for two years. They had a pretty bad breakup, and they worked for a long time to establish a friendship. Alex values the friendship because they overcame a lot and are now very close.

Mark is jealous and doesn't trust Alex—or Paul—and he tries to talk to Alex about it. Alex, on the other hand, feels it is entirely Mark's problem and that he should be left alone. This becomes a problem for Mark, but Alex doesn't believe that Mark has a reason to be suspicious because, in his mind, the relationship with Paul is over and they are simply friends.

Mark tells Alex he would feel more comfortable if he would introduce him to Paul and they could all go out once in a while. Alex insists that Mark is wrong and says that if he doesn't trust him, he might as well end the relationship. Mark backs down, but he tells Alex that his actions come across as secretive.

In general, you do give up some autonomy in a relationship, including the freedom to go where you want and when you want without considering your partner. But it is important to see that in this situation both partners are "right." Alex is right that Mark should trust him because he wouldn't cheat on Alex. But Mark is also right not to trust someone who refuses to tell him where he is going and turns down his requests to meet his ex, which would alleviate his concerns. Because this issue is getting so heated and they are so angry with each other, Alex and Mark don't always wait to get home to have arguments about certain issues. Occasionally, they argue in front of friends, as this Red Flag considers.

⚑ RED FLAG: *Not Keeping a Lid on Conflict*

A couple may be heading for trouble when they can't keep a lid on arguments. You are creating uncomfortable situations when your arguments take place in front of other people. It also means that neither of you can wait, that you must resolve your differences right away.

Getting back to the issue of right and wrong, when you and your partner are both right but you think that the other person is wrong, where does this leave you? As differences of opinion arise, start with the assumption that your partner has a valid point of view. You are then able to shift your focus to thoughts and feelings, which is where the solution lies. For Alex, as for most couples, the shift allows him to consider Mark's feelings and to think less about who is right. Feelings are often not based on what is considered rational. However, Mark's mistrust has its roots in his fear that Alex will leave him for the on-again, off-again relationship with his ex. Mark has two legitimate concerns: "If Alex and I have a big fight, will he go back to his ex?" and "If their relationship was on-again, off-again, will our relationship go the same way, and when he's off with me, will he go back to Paul?"

Mark fears that Alex will have sex with Paul, or that he might even leave him, fears that are fueled by Alex's secretive behavior. Eventually, Mark realizes he can't stay in the relationship if Alex and Paul's friendship continues. In the middle of an argument, Alex tries to prove that Mark has nothing to worry about by telling him that Paul asked him to have sex and he turned him down. Instead of proving his point, the new disclosure inflames Mark because now he knows what Paul wants.

It's possible that if Alex and Mark had been able to discuss their feelings rather than focus on being right, they could have saved themselves from this emerging threat. If Alex had included Mark when he and Paul got together, Paul might not have had the chance to hit up on Alex. Even if Mark wasn't always around, Paul might have developed a separate friendship with Mark, and he may not have wanted to betray his new friend by coming on to Alex. Should Paul have hit up on Alex anyway, Mark could have felt secure enough to know that Alex's feelings for Paul were platonic and therefore Paul was not a threat to the relationship. This could have avoided the situation in which Mark now feels the need to demand that Alex end his friendship with Paul. Alex reluctantly agrees, which causes him to feel resentful.

Look at Your Differences in a Positive Way

Early on, it's easy to feel threatened as differences appear. Think about your differences. How can you frame them in a positive way? One way to do this is to take advantage of what each person brings into the relationship. For example, if you both enjoy being sociable but your partner doesn't like calling people to get together or plan movies, dinners, and so on, then you can be more of the social planner.

Let's say you have organizational and financial skills but no interest or talent when it comes to decorating. You can leave it up to your partner to determine the paint colors for the walls, select rugs and furniture, and decorate the rooms. When you add up your differences, you will see that you gain much more by being in a relationship than by being alone. Viewing your differences synergistically can create an atmosphere that allows you to accept and appreciate your differences.

Cooperate and Share Power

Cooperation seems basic, but figuring out how to cooperate with your partner is not. The challenge is to feel like a team. This in turn will affect your ability to do everything from living day-to-day to making it through rough times. Some issues require compromise. For example, you need to compromise on how clean your place should be (although you may have had many discussions and disagreements about it). However, cooperation is more than compromise. Sometimes compromise ends up causing both of you to feel you didn't get what you wanted. When you cooperate with each other, compromise isn't necessarily the solution.

Part of cooperation includes willing to be led; that is, be willing to do some activities simply because you know your partner wants to do them. Take the lead at other times. One option is take turns or find creative solutions. Think about this as you read about how Jason and Gregory work through a situation about an upcoming vacation.

CASE STUDY: *Jason and Gregory*

Jason and Gregory have two very different preferences for a vacation. Jason likes to explore and see the sights, and Gregory's ideal getaway is to lie on a beach, sip a cold beverage, and read a book.

Two months before their second anniversary of living together, Jason asks Gregory whether he wants to go to Maui for their anniversary. Gregory asks Jason what he'll do when they get there. Jason says he'd be okay with a little beach time, but he wants to spend most of his time exploring, going on a helicopter ride, biking, and hiking.

Gregory is unable to bike or walk long distances because of a recent foot injury; he can take the helicopter ride, but that's all he can do for exploring. Besides, he likes to lie on the beach. Jason suggests that they time their trip to coincide with that of another couple they know—Joe and Elliot—who also want to go to Maui. Joe enjoys seeing the sights and Elliot likes the beach, so Jason and Joe can explore while Gregory and Elliot spend time on the beach.

They agree to spend some of their time in Maui alone together, some of it together with their friends, and some separately with each of their friends. This way, Gregory and Jason will both get what they want without compromising.

As this situation illustrates, cooperation often takes creativity, and if Jason hadn't thought about timing their trip to coincide with their friends' vacation, Gregory would have been stuck alone on the beach, which would be no fun for him. Or Jason would have tried to drag him around, and Gregory could have damaged his injured foot. They agree that from now on the ideal way to travel will be with another couple or a small group of friends so that they can each find something they want to do with at least one other person.

In a related item, Jason makes more money than Gregory, so he could have tried to pressure Gregory to do it his way. In this situation, cooperation is tied to sharing power because the person with more power can more easily refuse to cooperate. At the same time, the partner with less power can feel intimidated and devalued or believe he is contributing less to the relationship.

To reverse this trend, the person with more power can share it, and the person with less can increase his sense of power in the relationship. To illustrate how to bring the "power gap" closer together through cooperation, consider Jason and Gregory's next situation.

CASE STUDY: *Jason and Gregory*

Jason's salary is considerably higher than Gregory's. Nonetheless, they work well together around the issue of money. Jason, who has more financial wealth and therefore more power to make financial decisions, has taken the responsibility to equalize the power as much as possible. In addition to checking in with Gregory about vacations and paying a proportional share of their income toward the mortgage, Jason also does not pay every time they go out to dinner. Instead, Jason takes Gregory to expensive places; but when Gregory asks Jason out to dinner, Jason is treated, no questions asked. Also, with every decision that has a financial implication, Jason consults Gregory. These strategies help Gregory maintain his dignity and a sense of personal power in the relationship.

As this example illustrates, the person with more money has more to do when it comes to sharing power. Jason could have insisted on paying for all their dinners, tried to get his way about vacations, and left Gregory off the mortgage; but he is aware of how it would affect their relationship. Cooperation and sharing power are both achieved at the same time.

Do's and Don'ts for Increasing Intimacy

You can behave in certain ways toward your partner to enhance intimacy. But you also have the potential to create emotional distance. Here's a list of don'ts, followed by the do's, to help you create an atmosphere of safety and trust.

The Don'ts

Don't manipulate your partner.

You can run into trouble by trying to get your partner to do what you want through manipulation. For example, if he smokes in the house and you want him to smoke outside, manipulation includes coughing when he lights up in the house, putting ash trays outside, or hiding his cigarettes in the hope you will get what you want. Rather than manipulate your partner, be direct when you make a request. A direct way to approach your partner is to ask him to smoke outside.

Don't complain to friends and family about your partner.

It's human nature to tell people when you're unhappy with something. When your partner upsets you, naturally you want validation and support. When you talk about problems in your relationship to friends and family, however, you influence how they feel about him. In particular, they may start to become protective of you and resent him for the hurt he's causing you. They may start to dislike him, and he will sense this and become uncomfortable around them.

When you complain about your partner, you unknowingly create a wedge between your partner and your friends and family. For every complaint you make about him, mention several positives. In an ideal world, you might be able to work out challenges or problems in your relationship without letting on to friends or family that there's a problem. However, you need reality checks, outlets, and support to help you work through relationship challenges, so balance it out by telling them the good things he does.

Be aware that you may be violating his trust by talking to others about your problems. To maintain good boundaries, let your partner know what you talk about with others. If he takes issue with what you discuss with them, try to find a balance you're both comfortable with. But it's not reasonable to insist you can't talk to anyone.

Don't ask your friends or family to referee your arguments.

Although your relationship can't be closed off from comments to friends and family, it's insulting if, when you are with others, you say, "See what I have to live with?" Your friends will be uncomfortable when you place them in awkward situations. When you ask people to referee, you make your relationship their business. There's a considerable likelihood they will later be accused of taking sides. That's why most people feel awkward about commenting on disagreements. Soliciting other people's opinion in a quarrel, arguing over who's right or wrong, and making mean-spirited comments to one another in front of other people creates emotional distance between you as a couple and your friends.

Don't say "You are" followed by a negative word.

Avoid hurtful comments beginning with "You are" followed by words such as "lazy," "uncaring," "self-centered," or "stupid." Despite your intention not to harm him, these statements can cause him to feel hurt, angry, and resentful. He may withdraw, become defensive, or verbally strike back at you. One of several things may be happening here. You may be trying to change him in some way. You may feel competitive or jealous, and demeaning him is your attempt to even the score. You may feel righteous, but it comes with a cost to intimacy.

Instead, consider what you would like to accomplish. When you want him to change an aspect of his behavior, talk about what he's doing, and then let him know how you feel about it. Instead of indulging in jealous or competitive behavior, talk about your feelings. You can begin with, for example, "There's something I need to get off my chest." If your feelings seem too overwrought compared to what's going on, look inside yourself for what's going on. Although you are reacting to something he's doing, you may also be reacting to your earlier experiences and people in your life.

Don't give your partner the Silent Treatment.

The Silent Treatment is an indirect way to let your partner know you're unhappy with something he has done. When you give your partner the Silent Treatment, you may be reacting to a family motto: "When someone does something to hurt me, he needs to be punished."

When you treat your partner this way, he may grow anxious and try everything he can to sooth your hurt feelings. On some level, this may be the response you're after. The Silent Treatment is likely to trigger his fears of abandonment, and he will do everything he can to not upset you further. Your partner will probably do what you want him to do, but it will cause resentment.

Giving him the Silent Treatment will also cause both of you to become increasingly frustrated. Your frustration is actually an opportunity to become more direct with your communication. Be aware of what you want to communicate. Instead of giving him silence, be direct with your anger. Likewise, should your partner give you the Silent Treatment, call it what it is and refuse to give up your power by allowing him to manipulate you. Tell him you will be happy to talk to him when he's ready, but in the meantime you are going to wait until he comes to you as you go on about your daily life.

Don't always react at the time something happens.

You shouldn't necessarily let your partner know how his actions affect you at the moment of an incident. For example, when you're angry, consider not expressing it until the anger has dissipated to the point where you are able to talk to him in a normal tone of voice. Take a walk, cool down, or just breathe. Instead of just wanting your own voice to be heard, listen to what he has to say. On the other hand, you don't want to wait for more than a few days because your partner will either forget what happened or remember the incident in a different way.

When it comes to sex, the best place to bring up the issue is at lunch, over coffee, or any time other than when you're having sex. At the time, it's okay to give him some directions ("Put your hand here," or "Harder, harder!"). But wait until later to talk to him so that you reduce the possibility that your request gets in the way of your sexual enjoyment or comes across as criticism.

The Do's

Do compare what you intend to say with what you actually say.

Be sure that what you intend to say matches how you come across to your partner. Communication can become bogged down in three ways: a problem with the sender, with the receiver, or with the message itself. When you, the sender, don't say what you intend to say, the receiver isn't going to get the correct message no matter how well he can try to infer what you said. When the receiver misunderstands what you're saying, he further distorts what is being said by interpreting the message incorrectly.

The problem may not be with the actual communication but with how you come across and the way he perceives it. The way you convey the message, your body language, and your past experiences all affect the message. Therefore, find out whether your partner understands what you're saying by checking it out with him. During important discussions, ask him to clarify what he thought you said by summarizing your main points. If he's having trouble following you, break your communication into smaller parts when discussing important subjects. Also, turn off the television and move away from the computer. Try to have as little distraction as possible when you talk.

Do respect your partner's boundaries.

In chapter 3, I mentioned boundaries as they relate to what people reveal about themselves, but they also include what people do. Opening your partner's mail, listening to his voice-mail, and reading his e-mail is an invasion of his privacy. If you're feeling distrustful in some way, instead of violating his rights by snooping, talk to him about how you're feeling. If, on the other hand, he's stepping over your boundaries by invading your privacy, work toward getting to the real issue of trust instead of focusing on his activities. Meanwhile, take steps to protect your privacy. If he accuses you of being secretive, let him know that privacy and secrecy are two different things. This area revolves around trust, so it's important that at some point you sit down to talk about the real issue.

Do work toward the underlying issue when you have a problem.

As with the example of the issue of trust underlying snooping, try to look for the underlying issues, or themes, for challenges. Note that, quite often, ongoing disagreements are stand-ins for deeper issues. One clue that this is happening is when you have a big argument and then, three days later, neither of you can remember what the fight was about.

Underlying themes include power struggles, insisting that you're right, and refusing to share power. To find these underlying issues, look for patterns in your disagreements. For example, if your disagreements revolve around whose way are you're going to do something, then the deeper issue is probably about control. Arguments about going out with friends, hanging out with an ex, and questioning who you are with and where you're going has a theme of trust. If disagreements revolve around who is spending what amount of money, the issue is probably about power. These underlying issues are not mutually exclusive.

Do please your partner.

Provide your partner several reminders that you're thinking about him. Bring him a gift without waiting for a special occasion. Offer him affection, such as a kiss or a hug when he's least expecting it. E-mail or text him during the day with a sweet message. Learn what your partner enjoys most, whether it's taking a walk in the park or getting together with friends, and occasionally initiate plans to do them. Pleasing your partner should be part of your relationship. Likewise, he should want to please you. When he does, show him your appreciation. By saying "Thank you," you can go far toward maintaining intimacy.

Do tell your partner when he makes you feel good.

Just as you create emotional distance by making negative "You are" statements, positive ones can increase closeness. You don't need to become obsequious, but tell your partner when he makes you feel happy, secure, or special. Try saying something as simple as, "You're so thoughtful." Even more powerful is to describe what he did and then explain how it affected you. Let's say your partner throws you a surprise birthday party. Afterwards, thank him and tell him you realize how much work it must have been to contact everyone, to book the restaurant, to create a ruse to get you to where you needed to be, and to get everything set up. At the same time, let him know how special it makes you feel.

Putting It Together

To deepen intimacy successfully in the early years of a relationship, the focus should be on developing a sense of teamwork, seeing beyond right and wrong, and letting go of trying to control your partner. You continue to grow as a couple as you accomplish the goals of sharing power and cooperating with each other. Though you're making some big adjustments, you have not finished. New challenges lie ahead, especially if conflict and emotional distance have become more common. In the next two chapters, we examine the origins of potentially harmful relationship dynamics, ways they interfere with intimacy, and how to challenge them successfully.

CHAPTER 7

Understanding Relationship Dynamics

WELL INTO YOUR relationship, you may have developed some ongoing issues that have become increasingly difficult to work through. If you sweep these issues under the rug or argue without resolving them, being at odds can lead to frustrating communication patterns. These patterns can evolve into harmful relationship dynamics and result in emotional distance. To understand the challenge of dynamics, in this chapter we consider a definition of relationship dynamics; examine the origins of these dynamics; and look at common types that may be affecting your relationship.

Defining Harmful Relationship Dynamics

Throughout the discussion of relationship dynamics, consider the following:

1. *Your partner expresses certain qualities and traits through what he says and does.*
2. *His behavior causes you to have a strong emotional response. At the beginning of the relationship, the emotional response was positive. Over time, it changed.*
3. *As your frustration and anger grow, you get locked into problematic ways (patterns) of relating to each other. The overall pattern is a fluctuation of emotional closeness and distance.*

4. *These patterns of communicating become a dynamic. As the patterns become well established, it causes both of you to become emotionally distant.*

It's challenging to understand how these four items apply to your relationship, but they are *vital* to working through relationship challenges. To begin, early in your relationship, the way you handled conflict influenced your feelings toward each other. These feelings in turn influenced how you tried to resolve future conflict. Later on, the conflicts, subsequent feelings, and attempts to feel close again become a pattern of communication. As the pattern becomes ingrained, threats to intimacy arise from ongoing, unresolved struggles; in turn, these struggles become barriers to intimacy. Your relationship can develop a vicious cycle that is difficult to overcome. See diagram 7.1 for an illustration of this phenomenon.

A. PRIOR TO THE EMERGENCE OF DYNAMICS (PATTERNS)

How you handled conflict

Feelings

B. ONCE PATTERNS WERE ESTABLISHED

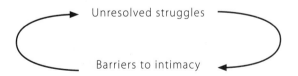

Unresolved struggles

Barriers to intimacy

DIAGRAM 7.1: VICIOUS CYCLES OF CONFLICT

How Attempts to Resolve Problems Can Become Part of Dynamics

Attempts to handle challenges can become incorporated into relationship dynamics, making them set firmly in place. For example, when you withdraw in an effort to let your partner know you're unhappy with him, your partner may feel threatened. A dynamic can occur in which your partner alternately reconnects and backs away when he feels as if he were walking on eggshells.

Another way of trying to resolve your differences that solidifies these patterns is when you need to settle them immediately. When urgency causes you to bring up something as you're going to bed, on the phone while you're at work, or out to dinner with friends, it only serves to concretize them. Telling your partner why he behaves in certain ways, name calling, and identifying his traits are other ways that existing patterns become solidified. You add fuel to the fire when you tell him he's moody, lazy, stupid, or crazy.

Projection and Dynamics

A complicating factor that relates to relationship dynamics is projection. When you assume you know what motivates your partner to behave a certain way, not only might you be wrong but you might be saying more about yourself than about your partner. Projection can occur in three ways. The first way is when you don't like certain parts of your personality or ways you behave, such as being absent-minded, jealous, or petty. Then you simultaneously deny their existence as you place them on your partner.

To illustrate, let's say you have a history of getting back at your partner when he does something that hurts you. You feel justified in retaliating not only because he hurt you but also because you believe you need to show him how it feels. Let's say your partner does something to you that hurts badly. You tell him he did it because he's retaliating. That's projection, because until he tells you why he did it, you're making the assumption; and, in fact, it's how you would have reacted to his hurting you.

The second way is when you assume what he's thinking about *you*. For example, let's say you are at dinner with your partner and you knock over a glass of water. You look at your partner and your first reaction is to think that he's thinking you're stupid or clumsy. Your assumption of what he thought actually belongs to you. You're the one who thinks you did something stupid or clumsy, and you transferred that thought onto him.

The third form of projection is subconsciously placing the image of mother and father, siblings, or someone else from your past onto your partner. When you transfer these images onto him, you assume that his thoughts or motivations behind his actions are the same as those of an important person from your past. Strong feelings become activated because you feel a threat to your well-being (or to the relationship itself).

To illustrate by expanding on the example of retaliation, let's say you grew up in a family whose members retaliated for perceived wrong-doings. In your relationship, you may suspect that your partner's motivation for doing something is to hurt you or at least he doesn't have your best interests at heart. Similarly, your family may have believed that when a family member did something wrong, retribution was the norm (as opposed to forgiving the offender or learning from the situation).

When your partner does something that hurts you, don't assume it was done in retaliation for something you did to him or for any other reason. Rather, check things out with your partner and accept his answer at face value. If you cannot take what he says at face value, then deeper dynamics related to honesty and trust are at work. As you become aware of your projections, you no longer need to protect yourself and come to accept, know, and express who you really are. Getting closer to him is then easier because you're less afraid of being your authentic self, complete with acceptance of all parts of yourself, both good and bad.

Determining When Dynamics are Emerging

You can discover when a dynamic is surfacing based on the emotional charge you get when you have certain relationship interactions. They can feel like walking into emotional landmines, and the feelings you experience as a result of his actions are larger than the situation itself. Examples include exploding with anger, feeling a horrendous sense of abandonment, or developing intense insecurity. Use these strong feelings as information that you're probably reacting to issues beyond what is happening at the moment. Deep beneath the surface, what he does to you not only activates strong feelings but also alters the way you feel about yourself. Suddenly and without warning, you can be a bad boy, a humiliated brother, or a weak son.

Use strong reactions (feelings) as a way to uncover your relationship dynamics.

Another way to uncover relationship dynamics is to consider when a pattern of communication leaves you both feeling distant and angry. You can become so entrenched in your patterns that when you are asked to describe what is causing the problem, you will say it's your partner's fault, and he would say the same. You are essentially holding up a fractured mirror to each other. In his parallel view, your partner would blame you, be defensive, and feel as angry and hurt as you feel.

Not all dynamics lead to relationship challenges. Some dynamics are positive and contribute to the well-being of the relationship. Being respectful and courteous are two examples of positive dynamics. But positive dynamics aren't what can get you into trouble. The important thing is to think of your relationship dynamics as a separate entity.

Other than challenges such as alcohol and drug addiction and domestic violence, nearly every challenge couples encounter involves relationship dynamics. (Dynamics could be involved with these more serious issues as well, but it's better to approach these problems as individual issues rather than relationship issues. I take these up in chapter 11).

Let's say you have had several relationships. If the problems that surface are similar, and, as important, the feelings you experience seem familiar, you are experiencing relationship dynamics that probably originated in childhood. You can examine your past by working through your present relationship challenges. But you must first go to the past to figure out how it all started.

Origins of Relationship Dynamics

You may believe that relationships are difficult because you didn't have visible role models while growing up (i.e., out gay male couples). However, your family of origin is the most powerful influence on all adult relationships. Your caregivers taught their children (gay and straight) directly and indirectly what intimacy looks like. Your perceptions regarding how they treated each other—and you—have the most profound impact on your capacity for intimacy.

The first six or seven years of life have a great deal of influence on the quality of your adult relationships. Another critical time is your teen years, which is the time of your budding sexuality. Many of my beliefs about the origin of relationship dynamics stem from the work of Alfred Adler, who was the founder of the school of psychology known as Individual Psychology, which has had a large influence on the humanistic and psychodynamic psychology that many psychotherapists practice today.

First, briefly consider the first few years of your life. When you were a baby, you were pure emotion. When you needed a diaper change, you cried from the discomfort. Hungry or thirsty? You cried and screamed for someone to get you something NOW. When someone cooed at you, you smiled happily. You didn't think you were happy.

You just were. You didn't think about being hungry. You didn't even know what hungry meant. You just were.

From the time when all you did was *feel* to the time you started to *think*, you were developing a tremendous attachment to your caregivers. Unknown to you, your attitudes and beliefs about relationships were already forming. Were your needs met with warmth and tenderness? Or were your caregivers anxious when you cried, or worse, neglectful or abusive? How did you handle these overwhelming feelings of dependence in the context of these caregivers who controlled your very existence? The way you were raised in your day-to-day life strongly influences your current relationship dynamics, which some call your ""attachment style."

An important discovery during the first couple of years of life is separating "me" from "you." Before this awareness, everything is "me" or an extension of "me." When you look at your early years this way, you have an easier time understanding why children blame themselves for family problems, including divorce. Although no one knows exactly when babies develop the ability to think, what is certain is that by the time you were three or four years old, you started to figure out what life is about. Not what your own life was about, but life for everyone, because it was the only world you knew. Whatever was going on with your family, there was a time when you believed that all families were this way.

The quality of your attachments to other people was gelling at this early age. At the time, you perceived your caregivers to be your gods. They fed you, clothed you, provided shelter for you, and were charged with raising you. You were truly powerless, and it was only through their care that you survived. Thus, you developed natural *feelings of inferiority* because you started out literally being inferior. You had to be taken care of, closely supervised. You were dependent on your caregivers for everything for the first several years of your life.

Fully functional parents (there are none) would have the natural ability to raise their children so that they feel esteem, confidence, and a sense of mastery. More likely, some messages from caregivers, teachers, and siblings caused you to feel proud of yourself, but others fueled feelings of inferiority. However, even messages that were supposed to have given you a sense of self-esteem could have had a negative impact. For example, if your parents used the term "good" to describe you or your activities without telling you what it was that made you or your activities "good," the praise was meaningless and it could have led to shame. "They believe I'm a good boy?" the child might think. "I just thought about hitting my brother again! And what if they find out that I spilled milk on the carpet a few minutes ago?"

As another example, consider this statement: "That's a beautiful painting." Although intended to make a child feel proud, the word "beautiful" does not mean nearly as much as if the parent had said, for example, "Wow. You painted a house here, and here's our dog, and there's the blue sky with some white fluffy clouds." A child can look at it and say to himself proudly, "Yes, I did that. That makes me good [skillful] at painting."

What about those behaviors that they wanted you to change? Unfortunately, parents who want to teach their children lessons or be better people can inadvertently cause fear, self-loathing, and shame. For example, think about the impact on you when you were a boy and you cried. Your parents might have said "Big boys don't cry" or, worse yet, "Crying is sissy" or "I'll give you something to cry about."

Likewise, when you were mad at your parents, you were probably scolded for getting angry, with the overall message that getting angry or hating your parents makes you a bad person. These actions caused you to feel ashamed, or to go into what I call "shame spirals" (falling into emotional pits with the thoughts "I'm a bad person" or "I am damaged goods"). To increase feelings of esteem, your parents should have said, "Let it out" and "It's okay to cry." They should have validated your anger by saying, "I can see why you're mad at us. I'd be mad too," or, simply, "I'm sorry."

By the time you were six or seven years old, the view of yourself became more solidified. You probably felt a sense of mastery in some areas and a sense of failure in others. You adopted a moral code based on your family's view of the world, and you started to see the world as an emotionally safe or somewhat unsafe place to be.

What happened as you started to feel "different," before you realized you were gay? You had to develop ways of coping with feeling different. These strategies may have been adaptive when you were a child but, when you reached adulthood, they interfered with intimacy. If you became isolated and retreated to books, or simply to your bedroom, think about how this reaction could transform into a form of withdrawal as an adult: the Internet, work, alcohol, and isolation.

If you were told that homosexuality is bad, and if you were teased or ostracized by peers during the time you were forming your sexual identity (teen years), your feelings of inferiority would naturally grow. Feelings of shame would multiply during this time, and the thought that others might know who you were attracted to would be horrifying. Similar to being a child and developing coping strategies for dealing with your family, you likewise developed ways to cope with a secret. Again, coping strategies that were adaptive at that time, strategies that included dealing with a horrible secret, can feed relationship dynamics.

Coping strategies are closely connected with your larger view of yourself. How you see yourself is in turn part of your worldview, which is your core beliefs about yourself, other people, and the world. As you look inside some of the deepest and most sensitive areas, you are taking a big step forward in developing the capacity for changing your dynamics. To that end, here's an exercise to help you uncover your worldview.

★ EXERCISE: MY WORLDVIEW

Complete the following sentences. Stick with the first ideas that come to your mind and don't over-think it.

- *I am a person who is …*
- *Other people are …*
- *Other gay men are …*
- *The world is …*

How did you finish the sentences? Do you see yourself as insecure or shy? Are other people or gay men untrustworthy or only in it for themselves? Is the world a mean or cold place? As you look at your answers, ask yourself, "How did I become the way I am, view others the way I do, and see the world how I see it?" You adopted core beliefs about yourself and others as a child and then behaved as if they were true. This is known as your worldview, and we all relate to others with little to no awareness of it until our core beliefs are questioned. You play out these themes everywhere, but they appear mostly in your relationship, where the emotional stakes are the highest.

As you work on yourself and get to know what *motivates* you, you have the opportunity to gain insight into how your worldview has affected your relationship dynamics. For example, let's say you were the second-born in your family. Your older brother was the academic whiz kid and athletic star, but you struggled with your classes and had no interest in sports. Attempting to fit in is an unconscious process, and you simply knew you had to find a way to fit in with your family and be acknowledged in ways that were different from your brother's ways (unless you became his shadow, which is still an attempt to fit in). You were doing this to gain the love and attention of your parents. How did you learn to fit in? Did you become rebellious and attract attention by spinning out of control? Did you try to develop an artistic ability or another way to get the attention you needed, only to be discouraged because your activities weren't "manly'" enough? Did you try to be perfect?

While you are thinking about your family history and its connection to dynamics, take a moment to think about how your family dealt with intimacy. Could you talk about anything on your mind? How much respect did your parents show for each other and for you? Were they openly demonstrative with their affection with each other? With you? Did your parents trust you? Think about some of the major feelings you had as you were growing up. Did you develop a fear of abandonment or rejection? Were you criticized a lot? Did you feel small (shame) when you were criticized?

Now, think about the dynamics and feelings in your relationship. Do they feel similar to the ones you had when you were a child? Does your view of yourself change when your partner is upset with you? Use the answers to these questions as information to understand the link between the past and present. You may be reacting to your childhood experiences more than to what's currently happening.

You unconsciously carry your worldview with you until adulthood, complete with the coping strategies you developed while you were growing up. Feelings of inferiority, along with your attachment style, bring about challenges related to intimacy. At first, these strategies worked for you because they helped you to survive. However, if they led to isolation, unhealthy habits, or limited ways of viewing relationships, these same coping strategies promote challenging dynamics as an adult. The more dysfunctional your upbringing, the more difficulty you have with future attachments (relationships). To illustrate how relationship dynamics have their beginnings in childhood, let's look at Alex and Mark's latest challenge.

CASE STUDY: *Alex and Mark*

A few weeks ago, Alex sent his automobile registration renewal in the mail. One day, Alex gets home from work and opens a letter from the Department of Motor Vehicles. It says that they are unable to renew it until an outstanding parking ticket has been paid. Alex recalls that he loaned his car to Mark about a month ago when Mark's car was in the shop.

When Mark arrives home, Alex erupts. He says he is fed up because Mark is irresponsible. Mark replies: "I don't know anything about the ticket." Alex says: "You're lying." Mark shoots back: "I'm not lying. Just shut up and leave me alone." Alex yells at him, listing several irresponsible things Mark has done since they got together. Mark walks away, and Alex follows him. Mark demands that Alex leave him alone as he runs into the bedroom and slams the door.

A few minutes later, Mark bursts out of the room. As he races by, Mark says: "You'll be sorry for this." Alex, unable to bear the horrible feeling he has in the pit of his stomach, chases after Mark to smooth things over. Alex pleads with him not to leave, and when Mark tries to leave through the front door, Alex stands in front of it; Mark pushes Alex out of the way and slams the door behind him. When Mark returns, as with the other episodes, neither of them talks about what's going on and they carry on as if nothing had happened.

Alex and Mark are finding themselves in an increasingly severe dynamic. When they have a fight, Alex raises his voice, Mark gets defensive and then withdraws, and Alex tries to soothe Mark's feelings (in actuality, to soothe his own). However, the dynamic is getting more severe because Mark is withdrawing in more dramatic ways.

Two hand-in-glove dynamics are happening. The first one relates to Alex's being a "good boy" when he was a child. When his parents weren't around, Alex was in charge of his younger brother, and when his brother made a mistake, Alex was held responsible. Alex therefore felt he needed to control his brother's actions. When his brother didn't listen to him, Alex yelled at his brother. He screamed at his brother because he'd panic, wanting to avoid being blamed or feeling ashamed when his parents stopped talking to him as a form of punishment. Alex was devastated by their silence, which he equated with a withdrawal of their love. So he would do anything, including yell at his younger brother, to try to avoid filling up with shame and feeling abandoned by his parents.

On the other end of this dynamic, Mark was spoiled as a child, and his parents repeatedly rescued him by letting him off the hook.

Mark's father often fell into rages; when he yelled, Mark would run into the basement to hide. Mark's father always felt guilty afterwards, so both parents overcompensated by protecting Mark and overindulging him. Mark soon learned he didn't have to deal with the consequences of his actions. As a young adult, he worried less about financial concerns, such as unpaid bills and accumulating debt, and his parents bailed him out. Although he has been doing better, he was still not nearly as responsible as Alex. The way each partner was raised created the relationship dynamic in which Alex cleans up after Mark's occasional messes, and then tries to control Mark by yelling at him. In spite of his perception that Mark is irresponsible, Alex has continued to bail Mark out, therefore allowing him to avoid the consequences.

Another dynamic that is occurring: When Alex yells, Mark goes to the bedroom or leaves the apartment. Mark withdraws because Alex's rage reminded him of his father's. He feels threatened and uses an old coping strategy, namely, running away. Alex can't stand feeling abandoned, so he needs to patch things up right away. As a result, they have two sets of relationship dynamics. This example also illustrates the hand-in-glove nature of relationship dynamics; the early childhood scene unconsciously being played out by Mark fits perfectly with Alex's childhood scene.

Common Types of Relationship Dynamics

Let's look at a few more types of dynamics, including pursuer-withdrawer, rescuer-wounded bird, pleaser-criticizer, and caretaker-carefree.

Pursuer-Withdrawer

Pursuers are highly sociable. They enjoy being with people and socializing. Think of the pursuer as a big lap dog who wants to be friends with everyone, wants to have people around a lot, and yearns to be loved, held, and appreciated. In contrast, think of withdrawers as cats. Withdrawers tend to be private, to need a lot of space. Able to take you or leave you, they want affection on their own terms and, when they get enough, they walk away. Sometimes, withdrawers become that way because they have been burned in previous relationships or they have learned to cope with being in a dysfunctional family by isolating themselves. They use the appearance of being aloof as a defense. More increasingly serious ways a withdrawer copes is by drinking or using drugs, working all the time, or having an affair.

The tendency to pursue or withdraw existed before the relationship and becomes more intense as each person plays off the other (the dynamic). The withdrawer has a strong initial attraction to the pursuer because he sees the other person being sociable and wants to be more like him. The withdrawer mistakenly believes he can gain this quality by being with someone who is outgoing and sociable. At the same time, the pursuer may be attracted to the "peaceful" withdrawer because his own life feels too much like a merry-go-round. Thinking he's become too superficial, he wants to be more of a homebody and have time with just one other person instead of always being in a crowd. He mistakenly believes he can do this by being with a quiet person.

Each person gets what he wants at first. The withdrawer is more involved with his partner's activities and the pursuer has the chance to recharge. After a while, the withdrawer realizes he needs more space than he's getting. The pursuer becomes confused and frustrated, perhaps not realizing what's happening as the withdrawer starts to pull back. He wants to be with the withdrawer, but the withdrawer wants space.

Fast-forward a couple of years. The pursuer complains that the withdrawer is not spending enough time with him. The withdrawer counters that the pursuer is smothering him. However, the withdrawer has a fear of attaching because he has had experiences in which other people betrayed or abandoned him. Ironically, pursuers continually push withdrawers away by becoming what the withdrawer sees as overbearing. In the extreme, they can become like Alex and Mark and play out the dynamic in dramatic ways.

Rescuer-Wounded Bird

With this dynamic, the rescuer finds men who don't have their act together, make little money, or have a drug or alcohol problem. The rescuer sees a wounded person instead of a whole person: Someone to take under his wing. Sometimes, the rescuer sees a reflection of his own distraught youth in his partner. Rescuing someone else can be an unconscious wish to be the one who should have been taken care of. Alternatively, he may want a symbolic son or little brother to take care of.

In this kind of relationship, two themes tend to emerge. First, the person being rescued takes what his "rock" or "anchor" has to offer. The wounded bird could be looking for a sought-after education or a safe place to stay. The rescuer may also be simultaneously taking what the wounded bird is offering him, including the need to be needed or to take care of someone. Most of these relationships are extremely challenging because they "work" only when the partners remain in their positions. Once one partner or the other starts to realize what is happening and he begins to change, his partner finds it threatening. After getting what he needs, which could take a few months to several years, the wounded bird is "healed" and may leave the nest.

Pleaser-Criticizer

This dynamic has the pleaser, who usually starts out as the good son. The good son wanted to satisfy his parents, and now he will do anything to please his partner. As a child, the good son had to excel just to feel okay. What happens to good sons as adults? For one thing, they can't make mistakes, and so they become perfectionists. For perfectionists, a B grade is not good enough. It feels like an F, so when they don't get an A, they give up or won't even try.

Perfectionism is a cover-up for feeling inferior. When strong feelings of inferiority are out of the pleaser's awareness, he may find a critical partner who sees his mistakes as part of one's character rather than as a part of being human. When his feelings of inferiority are reinforced through criticism, the pleaser thinks, "No matter what I do, I'm not good enough."

The pleaser tries and tries, but, no matter what he does, the criticizer belittles his efforts because the criticizer is unhappy with him. A criticizer is someone who may feel entitled to being treated a certain way, and when others fall short of his expectations, he's going to let them know about it in no uncertain terms. He could also be an unhappy person, so no matter what the pleaser does, the criticizer can't be pleased.

Caretaker-Carefree

With this dynamic, one partner starts to take more responsibility than the other one. As this happens, the couple becomes ripe for conflict. Ironically, the way they disagree fuels the dynamic. To illustrate, consider the issue of responsibility for pets. The caretaker makes sure that the couple's pet is walked, vaccinated, fed, dipped, and has plenty of toys. The carefree partner may start out by being equally responsible; but because the caretaker talks more about it, the carefree partner's level of responsibility begins to slip, perhaps as a way of letting the caretaker know he doesn't like being told what to do. The caretaker gets angry because he is doing more than his share.

As the carefree partner waits the caretaker out, he will find that the caretaker—despite his nagging and pleading—ultimately takes care of the pet. This reinforces the idea in the carefree partner's mind that the caretaker is worrying enough for both of them, so he can then avoid worrying about it. At the same time, the carefree partner stops caring about the responsibilities and so he attends to them less.

Like most other dynamics, this pattern starts in childhood. Every child grows up with different levels of responsibility placed on him by his parents. Often, as with Alex, the oldest child is saddled with responsibility for the lives of his younger siblings. The oldest child therefore more easily slips into the role of caretaker. On the other hand, a child who grew up having less responsibility tends to feel less anxious and concerned. As adults, the caretaker grows more concerned and takes over as the carefree partner relaxes. He tells the caretaker, "You're too uptight. Don't get so worked up over it."

Other Types of Dynamics

Another dynamic starts with what's called "a splitter." During childhood, the splitter had a caregiver who was sometimes kind and at other times enraged; or he had one loving parent and another who was cold, distant, or abusive. The world of relationships would therefore seem uncertain. So that he can cope, the splitter develops a strategy by seeing people as "good" or "bad." When a person is good, the splitter forgets about the bad person; and when a person is bad, he forgets about the good person he once knew.

Because no one is entirely good or entirely bad, the splitter divides his partner into "good partner" and "bad partner." Because he divides his world into two, the splitter will want to be close to the good partner and at other times he will want to run away from the bad partner. Instead of seeing his partner realistically as a person with faults and virtues, the splitter uses his old coping strategy. When he's good, his partner is rewarded, and when he's bad, he's punished. Both partners alternatively feel loved and unloved.

Another dynamic stems from how a person's family of origin dealt with anger. Growing up in family where it's not okay to feel angry toward one's parents can lead to hiding natural feelings of anger and aggression because, in this person's worldview, such feelings are equated with a loss of love. He also translates this to mean: "When my partner gets angry with me, he doesn't love me anymore." This person may find someone who accommodates his worldview that it's not okay to be angry. They will suppress their anger with each other until it builds to the point where it can't be avoided.

A third dynamic arises when a person believes that the purpose of a relationship is to have someone fulfill his every need. Inevitably, his partner will disappoint and frustrate him. Emotionally wounded as a child, he may have the unconscious expectation that his partner can heal his childhood wounds. He's looking for stability and security and when his needs go unmet, power struggles develop; these result from his attempts to coerce his partner into meeting his needs by criticizing him, threatening to leave him, and manipulating him. When power struggles develop as a result of unmet needs, he may not be sure whether to flee or to keep trying to change his partner in some way (i.e., to meet his needs). It's unrealistic to find someone who can heal his early wounds, so he inevitably finds that his partner verifies his worldview that other people let him down.

Putting It Together

Detrimental relationship dynamics place intimacy at risk. However, many patterns in your current relationship started long before you met your partner. They were intact as you attempted to fit into your family of origin, received early messages about yourself, and observed your parents' role-modeling of relationships. These patterns were then reinforced by experiences with former partners. You bring the imprint of these memories and experiences to your current relationship.

Changing these dynamics is challenging, but it can be done by first understanding how they arose and by accepting responsibility for your part in creating them. Let's now consider additional tools to stop ongoing patterns of conflict and distance so that you can again feel close to your partner.

CHAPTER 8

Changing Relationship Dynamics

AS RELATIONSHIP DYNAMICS solidify, it's hard to see each other's point of view and try to find areas of agreement. That's why it's important to look underneath the issues that appear on the surface so that you can arrive at the real reasons your relationship has these patterns. Here we explore ways to overcome these patterns and improve your relationship.

When You Have "Tried Everything"

If you feel frustrated about trying to change locked-in patterns in your relationship, you probably haven't started looking inside yourself for answers to the questions just posed. For vexing relationship patterns, the first thing to do is stop looking to your partner to change and ask yourself what part you are playing in your relationship dynamics. However, asking yourself to change the way you relate to your partner is easier said than done. In fact, the bridge from "knowing" to "doing" can be the most difficult to cross. To find ways to react differently when you are faced with ongoing relationship patterns, consider the following:

- *As you change the way you communicate with your partner, overall communication will change.*
- *As your overall communication changes, ongoing patterns will start to shift.*

- *As the patterns adjust, your partner will respond differently.*
- *You will eventually bring out different qualities and traits in each other and your relationship dynamics will change.*

When I talk about changes in your partner, I'm not saying that you can change his personality. I'm referring to the way you react to each other, which influences your current relationship dynamics. Changing the way you and your partner relate to each other is like mastering a new skill, and tackling any new skill is challenging. You will make some progress, then take some steps back before going forward again. It will take time to become automatic. However, no matter how automatic your new responses become, you may fall back on old coping strategies when you are stressed out or blindsided. Therefore, don't think you are going back to your old ways when you occasionally slip.

In spite of knowing that your relationship could be better, changing your dynamics is difficult because *any* change is scary. When you interrupt the pattern, your partner may feel threatened; if this happens, he will try to make things go back to the way they were because he is afraid of change. He may even try to provoke you at levels you haven't seen before. As you think about how this could apply to your relationship, consider how Alex began addressing their pursuer-withdrawer dynamic.

CASE STUDY: *Alex and Mark*

After asking Mark several times to not withdraw, Alex realizes that if the dynamic is to change, he will have to change. As hard as this is for him, Alex doesn't chase after Mark the next time he runs into the bedroom. Mark doesn't emerge from the bedroom for an hour. Already, their relationship equilibrium is changing.

But Alex isn't prepared for what happens next. After another thirty minutes, Mark flies out of the bedroom with a packed bag and announces that he is going to stay at his friend Gary's house for the night. Alex's gut reaction is to panic, and before he can stop himself, he pleads with Mark not to leave. Mark relents. Alex doesn't realize until later that Mark had raised the stakes, which is why he fell into the old pattern of chasing Mark. Alex resolved that no matter what Mark did next time he was not going to pursue him.

After their next fight, Mark predictably runs into the bedroom and emerges an hour later with a packed bag. Alex still feels panicked, but he doesn't succumb to an immediate reaction. Instead, he takes a few deep breaths. As Mark is leaving, Alex says: "You know I love you and I wouldn't do anything to hurt you, but I am not going to chase you. You are free to stay wherever you want. Just remember I will have to start taking care of myself."

Mark arrives three hours later, but he comes back to an empty house. There is a note on the table: "I called Sherly to go to dinner and a movie, and I will be back by 10:30." Alex took care of himself for the first time and he feels proud of the way he handled the situation. He knows that if it ever happens again, he will fight hard within himself to not react in the old ways. Meanwhile, Mark has a couple of hours to be by himself. He is thinking for the first time about how his own actions create unnecessary drama and may tear them apart.

Changing Your Relationship Dynamics

You can change your relationship dynamics when you respond to what your partner is doing rather than automatically reacting to strong feelings he is activating from your past. To begin this shift, start by taking responsibility for your part in your relationship dynamics. If your relationship has a fixed dynamic, you have the power to change the way you react, just as Alex did. However, you need to take certain steps before making the adjustments.

One step is to realize that you are locked into a dynamic. This process can take some time. It's difficult to figure out how much of the problem is caused by you, how much stems from your partner, and how much is a result of the relationship dynamic. Be patient with yourself during the process of discovery. Changing a dynamic is difficult because you have to take the step of accepting responsibility for your part in it. Accepting responsibility means being aware of *how* you play a part in the dynamic as well as learning *why* you are contributing to it.

When you consider the origins of your part in the relationship dynamic, look to your childhood, young adulthood, and former relationships to determine where the seeds were sown. As you realize why you're contributing to the dynamic and get to the point where you understand what you're doing in the moment of a disagreement, you are able to be less reactive.

When Alex was a child, he *knew* that if he was a good boy and behaved properly, his parents wouldn't go away. He carried this mistaken belief with him into his current relationship. But when he uncovered what was happening inside, he understood that because he was reacting in an increasingly irrational manner as a result of his fear of abandonment, a relationship dynamic had become locked into place.

Mark knew he could always get what he wanted by manipulating Alex through withdrawal, so he used it in increasingly harsh ways. This is not to say that Mark is a bad person. He wasn't even conscious of what he was doing. In the last fight, when he realized that he could be destroying their relationship, Mark then had to figure out why he was behaving in this way.

Sure enough, it went back to a dynamic he had with his father, who, despite being proud about being the breadwinner of the family, felt guilty about being absent a lot and not being there for his children. Instead of dealing with his guilt, he belittled his children by raging. To counteract that, when Mark pouted or whined about anything, his father—along with his mother—would give in to his wishes. Mark later discovered that when he withdrew by becoming silent, his parents would ask him what was wrong and how they could help him. They would offer to take him shopping for a toy or to a movie. Mark got the attention he craved from his parents by withdrawing. When he threatened to run away, his parents did everything they could to mollify him. The behavior exhibited by Mark's parents was similar to Alex's; Alex tried to placate Mark as well.

Sometimes, as with Alex and Mark, it's difficult to untangle where your contribution is coming from because the dynamics can be ingrained and unconscious. But there are ways to unearth unconscious beliefs that are related to your family of origin. The following exercise is designed to help you uncover early family dynamics.

★ EXERCISE: FAMILY ARCHEOLOGY

One way to uncover your part in your dynamics is to become a "family archeologist." You don't need to think back to the days of your childhood if your family of origin still gets together for special occasions. When you go for a visit, if you find yourself in old patterns that arise after the pleasantries have worn off, step back and look at how your family members are treating you and each other. Decide beforehand that you will act as a witness to your family dynamics. Pay attention to your feelings and your usual reaction to those feelings, including how you feel about yourself, as well as your reaction to what's going on between your family members.

Afterwards, think about how those same dynamics play out in your current relationship. If you don't already know, you may be surprised by how similar they are. Once you have learned why you're reacting to your partner in certain ways and are able to maintain a higher level of awareness when it's happening, you have come a long way toward altering your relationship dynamics.

Take the time to discover how early family dynamics influence your current relationship patterns, but avoid using your childhood as an excuse. When your partner is upset with you and you react by telling him it's just the way you are, you are merely justifying bad behavior. Use what you are learning about your relationship dynamics and their origins in your childhood as a force for maturing, healing, and outgrowing them.

You need to have a lot of fortitude to withstand uncomfortable feelings that come from attempts to change long-standing patterns. Change is scary, and you are venturing into uncharted territory. If you're a pursuer or have a lot of insecurities about your relationship, you are especially courageous for taking the risk that the relationship will get worse before it gets better and, even more frightening, facing your fear that your relationship will end.

What does it take to develop courage? It usually takes some sort of outside support. Whether it is a family member, a therapist, or a good friend who supports your relationship and understands what is going on, you need to have an outlet for the uncomfortable feelings that result from trying to change your dynamics. Another way to develop courage is to tell yourself that you will by okay no matter what happens to your relationship.

At the point you consider making a change, you are probably asking yourself whether you can continue to live this (old) way. If you're not willing, but leaving is not an option, you have little to lose by making changes within yourself, taking risks by changing the way you relate to your partner, and allowing the consequences to fall where they may. In fact, one risk of not changing yourself is that, if you do end this relationship, the chances are good that you will find yourself in a similar situation with your next partner.

Once you have developed a plan to counteract your relationship patterns, remember that you are not going to do it perfectly the first time. You're learning a new skill. Do the best you can and fine-tune as needed to protect yourself and your feelings, put your needs on the same level as—and at times above—your partner's needs, and reassure your partner that the change does not spell the end of the relationship.

Ask Yourself, "What Are My Hidden Goals?"

Discovering your part in relationship dynamics includes learning the hidden goals stemming from ongoing relationship patterns. These goals are hidden because you may not be aware that you're doing this. Many times, a goal is to test your partner's loyalty, learn how much you can trust him, or find out what it would take for him to leave you. As an example, Mark's hidden goal was to gain Alex's attention and reassurance. He could have been direct had he allowed himself to be vulnerable, trusted Alex not to hurt him, realized that this is what he was doing, and recognized that he could go about asking for reassurance in more direct ways.

To some degree, everyone has a fear of abandonment, which gives rise to the need for reassurance. You don't need to have abusive parents to fear emotional or physical abandonment. Be sensitive to your partner's natural need for reassurance and recognize that whenever you threaten to leave your partner, you potentially create a harmful dynamic. As a result, he's going to put his defenses up and may continue to test you by arguing with you instead of asking for what he needs.

If you feel yourself resisting when you want to make a change in a relationship dynamic, ask yourself this: "If we didn't have this ongoing pattern, how would our lives be different?" If you are like most people, you will say you would have more peace of mind. The next question: "What am I getting out of this [your hidden goals]?" For some couples, the answer is that if life was peaceful, they would get to the more critical issues they have been avoiding. Ironically, fighting can be a way to avoid greater conflict! In the least, it can be a way of avoiding something more painful than what you're going through.

To answer the question about hidden goals, another explanation is that your relationship patterns are verifying your worldview. You may be acting in certain ways to bring out a particular reaction from your partner to verify your core beliefs about yourself, other gay men, and the world in general. Before the shift in dynamics, Mark's worldview was repeatedly verified by his ongoing conflicts with Alex.

Mark's worldview included:

- *I can get what I want by withdrawing my love (achieving his hidden goal of getting reassurance by manipulating Alex to run after him).*
- *Others cannot be trusted (which is reinforced by Alex's yelling at him).*
- *The world is unstable (verified by his increasingly dramatic attempts at controlling Alex by running into the bedroom and leaving the house).*

Alex's worldview included:

- *I have to be perfect for people to love me and I am responsible for other people's feelings (as indicated by his belief that he makes Mark leave, and therefore, he can make him stay).*
- *Other people mistreat me (verified by Mark's dramatic exits).*
- *The world is uncertain, except when I please others (the relationship returns to normal when he placates Mark).*

Let's turn to ways to change the various types of dynamics we discussed in the last chapter.

Changing Pursuer-Withdrawer Dynamics

For the Pursuer

The pursuer will have an easier time behaviorally but a harder time emotionally when changing the pursuer-withdrawer dynamic than the withdrawer. It's easier behaviorally because, as with Alex, when you stop pursuing, you are giving the withdrawer room to come forward. He will take more notice of the particular situation and broach the subject first or be the first to try to break the ice after a fight.

This is exactly why it's emotionally very difficult for the pursuer to stop pursuing. You're pursuing because you want to restore closeness and don't want to live with feelings of uncertainty. You also don't want your partner to remain angry with you. But it's also exactly why you must stop pursuing if you wish to change the dynamic. You inadvertently push him away when you pursue to restore closeness, and you prevent him from taking responsibility for getting closer to you.

For the Withdrawer

Resist the urge to withdraw from conflict and use more direct ways of expressing your feelings. Start off with something small. For example, ask him to rinse his dishes after he eats. As you become more comfortable with conflict, work your way up to larger issues. Remind yourself, especially during periods of tension and conflict, that your actions are injecting an inordinate amount of drama into the relationship by igniting your partner's fear of abandonment—and it will only cause him to pursue, thus fueling the dynamic.

In more challenging situations, for example if your partner repeatedly yells at you, say something like, "I hear what you're saying, but reduce the volume." Or, "Keep the intensity, but lower your voice." Then, take a breath. Listen to what your partner is saying instead of walking away. You don't need to respond to something he says immediately. Tell him you want to think about it before responding. However, telling your partner you will think about it and then never approaching him is simply a creative form of withdrawal. So be sure to come back to him later in the day or the next day to let him know you're thinking about it or have a response.

Changing Rescuer-Wounded Bird Dynamics

For the Rescuer

When you have become a rescuer, you need to look inside yourself for the reasons you want to rescue another person. Your reasons may indeed be altruistic, and you may have your partner's best interests at heart. However, a rescuer can have more selfish reasons for wanting to rescue, and an honest self-evaluation is required. Is it easier to control a partner who has less power in the relationship? Do you need a trophy husband? Are you yearning to regain your lost or incomplete youth? These questions may seem harsh to nonrescuers, but they're likely to be spot on if you're a rescuer because you know on some level that you're doing it more for yourself than for your partner.

For the Wounded Bird

As you heal (i.e., grow and mature), you usually end up feeling caged in a relationship that you realize is based more on need than love. However, if you care for your partner and want to stay with him, let the rescuer down gently. If you try to regain your independence all at once, the relationship has a greater chance of imploding. Rather, take small steps to regain your independence. For example, tell your partner way in advance that you want to have dinner with a friend. As you make new friends, have him join you the first few times so that he feels less threatened by your new-found independence.

Meanwhile, start or continue on the road to wellness. If you want to go back to school, for example, now is the time to begin. Keep your partner involved by telling him about your desire. Take him to campus with you to pick up some information (or have him sit by your side as you peruse the Internet for online courses). Solicit his information and advice, not because you want to placate him, but to gain from the experience and wisdom he so happily shares with you.

Changing Pleaser-Criticizer Dynamics

For the Pleaser

You should readily be able to identify the direct line from your good-son role in your family of origin to your current role of pleasing your partner. When your partner activates your need to please, be aware of who you're actually responding to. Is it your mother? Your father? An early teacher or sibling?

What feelings is the criticizer activating in you? Usually the need to please is born out of insecurity. If that's true for you, work on yourself to build up your self-image. Surround yourself with good friends while reconsidering friends who bring out your feelings of insecurity or unworthiness—something I call "weed and feed." That way, you more easily inoculate yourself from a critical partner.

Try not to defend yourself. It may sound counterintuitive, but defending yourself just gives the criticizer more reasons to criticize. Rather, tell him you will think about it before responding. In the meantime, differentiate between criticism and justified feedback. If he doesn't like something you do, don't automatically label it as criticism.

For the Criticizer

Be aware you may be using your partner as an outlet for your own unhappiness. Of course, you aren't doing this consciously, but you may be "kicking the dog" rather than dealing with your own dissatisfaction. You may have placed your partner in the "not good enough" category. If so, instead of taking your frustrations out on your partner, make a conscious effort to work on improving your own life circumstances.

On the other hand, if your partner is the one with the "not good enough syndrome," place your attention on being sensitive to his feelings but not falling into a trap of being hesitant to talk about a subject because your partner says he's feeling criticized. When you have a legitimate complaint, be sure to speak up, but remember that other people want to hear what they are doing right a lot more than what they are doing wrong, and you shift the dynamic by emphasizing what pleases you.

Changing Caretaker-Carefree Dynamics

For the Caretaker

When anxiety and worry dominate you, it's very hard to back off from situations you know you could do better, faster, or more economically than your partner. Even more challenging, you don't want your partner to make costly mistakes, so you tend to step in instead of allowing him to accept the consequences of his actions.

You may have to sit on your hands occasionally (figuratively and literally) and let your partner make decisions, take action, and await the consequences, even when you *know* they may not turn out for the best. Especially if you are inclined to catastrophize, remember that much learning comes from trial-and-error; the outcome is almost never as bad as you think it will be. Don't forget that sometimes your partner needs to feel powerful and productive.

For the Carefree Partner

Become a container for your partner's concerns. As a good container, listen to your partner without responding angrily or defensively. As you stop reacting in old ways, you will draw from the secure part of yourself: This part realizes that no matter what he is doing or saying, you do not have to respond defensively or aggressively. You have the potential to become a calming force in the relationship.

If he accuses you of being standoffish or uncaring, tell him you do care about him but at the same time you are not going to allow yourself to fall into an old pattern. As you maintain a stance of acceptance and nonjudgment, you are creating a safe space for your partner to look at his issues, which makes you the ultimate container. This will happen because you are no longer fighting fire with fire, and he is forced to reconsider and take responsibility for his actions.

Putting It Together

Once you and your partner have realized that your patterns of communicating have become unproductive, you can stop them by increasing your awareness, taking responsibility for your part, and uncovering your hidden goals. In so doing, you and your partner are able to identify the deeper meaning beneath the surface conflict and tension. Regardless of the dynamics that have emerged, you can take specific steps to change the themes that originated in your past. But the past is only one source of relationship difficulties. The next chapter explores current obstacles to intimacy and ways to work through them so you can get closer.

CHAPTER 9

Negotiating Gay Relationships in a Straight World

MOST OF US live in a world that is unsupportive of our relationships. An unfriendly or hostile environment can silently enter and undermine our best intentions at developing intimacy. Consider the challenges we face amid homophobia and heterosexism. These include unsupportive family-of-origin members, workplace and other types of discrimination, and internalized homophobia. Also, growing up "male" in our culture includes being socialized to be aggressive, competitive, and unemotional. Let's consider these issues, how they impact your relationship, and how to overcome them.

Family of Origin

During your relationship, both your family of origin and your partner's family influence your relationship by being a resource and a stressor. Even when both families are generally accepting of your relationship, they can still be a source of stress. For example, one sibling is supportive but another one is homophobic and doesn't support you at all. Regardless of each family member's level of support, how you deal with your families and subsequently work through your issues is going to come up.

Supportive and Unsupportive Families

Supportive family members are those who embrace your partner as a member of the family. Because they regard you as any other (i.e., heterosexual) couple, they offer built-in validation of your relationship and a subtle public pressure to work out your differences. They view you as they would one of their straight adult children. Their expectations coincide with yours when it comes to considering your partner ahead of your family of origin. They respect your relationship, so it's relatively easy to navigate between your family of origin and your relationship and not feel trapped in the middle.

A supportive family of origin can strengthen the bonds between you and your partner. Your family can share in his successes, know the kind and thoughtful things he does for you, and want to have their own relationship with him as any other son- or daughter-in-law. You would naturally feel closer to your partner as you both take part in celebrations and milestones. He can also lean on your family for support during rough times. For example, when your partner suffers a loss of someone close to him, he will include your family members among the people who will help him ease his pain.

Unfortunately, most families of origin are not fully supportive. Let's say your family is openly opposed to your relationship for religious reasons. They devalue your relationship and don't consider your partner to be part of their family. If you have routine contact with them and have family traditions you are expected to attend, it can be even more difficult. Having a family who will not acknowledge that you have a legitimate relationship forces you to make uncomfortable decisions about how to handle many situations. They are placing you in a difficult position because at times you will have to choose between them and your partner. You may have to confront the reality that no matter how well your partner behaves toward your family, how polite or nice he is to them, he will receive nothing but icy stares, ostracism, or open hostility.

Unsupportive or hostile family members can place considerable strain on your relationship. Differences of opinion on how to handle your family can create divided loyalty. For example, you want your partner to understand why your family members are reacting the way they are. However, he's too angry to care why they are reacting negatively and can't believe you're not siding with him. Intimacy suffers as a result. Consider the range of support when David informs his family of origin that he's in a relationship with Roberto.

CASE STUDY: *Roberto and David*

After seeing each other for six months, Roberto, who is forty-one, and David, thirty-two, decide to announce their relationship to several family members. Roberto has already taken David to meet his family, and Roberto's family likes David. Recall that David recently came out to his family. David knew that his family's reaction would be mixed, so he writes letters to his family about their relationship.

One day, David gets a call from his mother, who turns out to be fairly supportive. Interestingly, she never mentions his father and David never asks. Later in the week, he gets an e-mail from his sister Janet. Janet is upset because her husband, John, is uncomfortable about David's new boyfriend being around their son, Charles. Charles used to visit his uncle David during the summers, and David treasures their time together. The news is upsetting to David.

However, David doesn't e-mail his sister back or call her to talk about the situation. He tries to be understanding of their position. Roberto, on the other hand, is outraged. As a result, he warns David that when he sees them, he won't speak to them. David, on the other hand, doesn't want to create a new problem for his family. He urges Roberto to reconsider, but Roberto refuses. This causes friction because Roberto is upset with David for not standing up for them. David doesn't know how to handle Roberto's reaction.

How could they approach this situation with less friction between them? For one, instead of looking at David as the source of the problem because he didn't tell his brother-in-law that his views are unacceptable, Roberto could express his anger and outrage yet still insist that when David came out to his family he was confronting them with a large issue that they'd have to work through—just as Roberto's family had to do years ago.

Roberto could recognize that both of them are victims here and, in doing so, place more of the problem on a society that discriminates against gay men. They could strategize about how to help David's family cope with having a newly out member of the family, perhaps sending a book to his sister and brother-in-law, such as *Loving Someone Gay*. They could arrange to visit David's family so that the relatives can get to know Roberto, which is often when a family's prejudgments begin to change.

Instead of using this situation as a wedge issue, Roberto could show more understanding for David's concern about keeping the peace with his family. David could be more understanding of Roberto's feelings by agreeing that his brother-in-law is behaving in a typically homophobic manner; David could also admit that he is not yet standing up to his family and so validate Roberto's view of his procrastination. They could both settle into the idea that coming out is a process for the people David has recently told, as much as it is for David, and that this is just one step in the process.

You can generally counteract your family's ignorance and homophobia when you place a boundary around your relationship; this means showing through your actions that your partner has the same worth as the heterosexual married spouses in your family. You would be protecting the relationship more than you'd need to if you had a supportive family. This means being willing to talk to your partner about various situations before you talk to members of your family of origin or decide what you want to do. During your talks, feelings need to be aired and validated. Make decisions about what you will and will not do as a couple, with a special emphasis on giving credence to the person who has the most passionate feelings about it.

On the other hand, if you have been out for a long time and your family remains unsupportive, be willing to sacrifice closeness with them for the sake of your relationship. When your family gives you a choice, you won't have to decide because you have already made a decision that your partner is your family. As a result, your feelings of intimacy with your partner won't be lost to ongoing conflicts stemming from your family. To the contrary, you and your partner can grow closer as you mutually support each other and make decisions as a couple about what to do when challenges with your family of origin occur.

Holidays and Special Occasions

Two of the most challenging times are holidays and special occasions. Unless there are extraordinary circumstances, most parents would never think of excluding their heterosexual children's husbands and wives from family functions. However, your family of origin may place special restrictions, such as requiring you to sleep separately when you come to visit or not being affectionate with each other in front of children. Or they may simply not invite your partner.

You and your partner have some potentially tough decisions to make. You may want to see your family of origin very badly during these times; for this reason only you may choose to go by yourself. However, you gain in spending time with your family what you sacrifice in closeness with your partner. Even though your partner may be completely supportive of your going alone to holidays and special events, the two of you are missing out on shared experiences.

If your parents exclude your partner or place restrictions on you, there is no need to accept this as final. Rather, view your family's demands as simply the starting point for negotiation. Let's say your family of origin refuses to invite your partner for the holidays the first year you're together (or the first year they learn about your relationship). When you say you won't attend without him and follow through, they are faced with a conflict they have to resolve. It becomes more of their problem than one for you and your partner, and even though you may miss them at holiday time, maybe next year, or the following year, they will invite both of you. Alternatively, invite them to your place for the holidays, or visit them by yourself at other times during the year.

Societal Challenges to Sustaining Intimacy

Your family of origin is only one influence on your relationship. Other outside factors can make your relationships more challenging. These factors include:

- *Discrimination*
- *Internalized homophobia*
- *Being socialized as male*

Discrimination

Discrimination is a stressor that you have to deal with as you attempt to sustain a long-term relationship. To begin, societal institutions such as the government, schools, religion, and the media support homophobia. To illustrate how discrimination can play out in your relationship, let's say your partner is in the closet at work. The situation puts stress on you because you and your partner do not have the same rights and benefits afforded to heterosexual couples, a situation that can leave both of you feeling marginalized. Additionally, you might judge your partner for staying closeted. In turn, you and your partner face situations and have feelings that will bring about disagreements, especially if you think your partner should be out and he disagrees. Ongoing disagreements around this issue can create tension and emotional distance.

The main source of the problem does not lie with your partner, although you may think it does. The problem stems from working in an environment that presents risks associated with being out of the closet. These risks to your partner include hitting a glass ceiling, being ostracized by coworkers, and getting fired.

If your partner is not out at work, it can create problems in your relationship when you judge him for it. Whether it is at work, with family members, or friends, it wouldn't be unusual if you were to become impatient with a partner who is living in the closet and to pressure him to come out. If you're able to place the blame where it belongs—on society and its failings—then your discussions about when to come out, and to whom, can be conducted with greater compassion and understanding. Each of you should be able to come out at a pace that is comfortable for you. Support each other about when to come out and what to do during situations that result from discrimination.

Internalized Homophobia

Internalized homophobia is discrimination turned inward. Every gay man has a certain amount of internalized homophobia because homophobia, like racism and sexism, pervades society at every level. No gay man escapes negative societal messages, and when you internalize these messages, it makes sustaining intimacy more challenging. When you become aware of your own internalized homophobia and work on reducing it, you are overcoming a significant barrier to intimacy.

To understand the origins of internalized homophobia, let's turn back to your youth. The two most important times when children learn what relationships "look like" are in early childhood and during your teen years. If you were heterosexual, every aspect of your upbringing would be supporting an interest in girls.

Not so if you were interested in boys. Your family and peers provided powerful messages to you as you grew older. As a teenager, your desire to be openly gay, or even questioning, may have been thwarted by parents, siblings, teachers, and friends. Feelings of inadequacy going into puberty were made worse, resulting in shame. Shame arose because you were attracted to other boys and because you were different. Maybe you were teased, bullied, called names, or were punched, kicked, or even beaten. As a result, you grew up feeling isolated.

To be intimate, you need to able to feel good about yourself as a man *and* as a gay man. You have to feel entitled to enjoy sex with another man. Although no one escapes internalized homophobia, you would have had to work through a significant amount of it to maintain intimacy. As you think about your own internalized homophobia, consider the following situation.

Let's say that you and your partner go to a mall that's mixed with gay and straight people. You try to hold your partner's hand, but he quickly pulls away. What started out as a happy venture could end up with both of you feeling emotionally distant. If your partner doesn't want to hold hands with you in public, what's going on? Although public displays of affection sometimes compromise your safety, your partner might pull his hand away because the stares or disapproval he may get from other people would make him feel uncomfortable.

In one way or another, internalized homophobia will surface at different times during your relationship. What do you do with this information, and how can you use it to increase your level of intimacy? As you identify internalized homophobia, you begin to see difficult situations more clearly. Not being fully out inhibits intimacy by creating stressful situations and conflict, but you can stop blaming each other for problems that originate with society. At the mall, you could have asked your partner how he was feeling instead of reacting angrily. Then you could have reminded yourself about how you used to feel as you were coming to terms with being gay and the shame you used to feel. By doing so, you'd have more patience with the process of his coming out.

Once you develop patience for your partner's coming out process, you will be more compassionate toward him.

Being Socialized as Male

As children, the way we were socialized to be "male" has a major influence on intimacy and communication. Families channel societal messages about what it means to be a man, and they tell us what is acceptable behavior for men and what is unacceptable. Being socialized as a male has its advantages in same-sex relationships. For example, boys are generally socialized to be independent. This is a relationship strength, especially when there are periods of emotional distance or when your partner is going through major changes. If you encounter a time when you need to be apart for an extended period, independence can be very useful.

Boys are taught to be assertive. As an adult, you realize it's okay to ask for what you want from your partner, and asserting yourself is usually the best way your partner is going to know what you want. Assertiveness means being able to ask for what you want and being able to take no for an answer. When you won't take no for an answer, however, you are crossing the line from being assertive to being aggressive, which inhibits intimacy. Overall, we were taught to adopt certain characteristics because they were necessary to becoming a man, but they can also create emotional distance. We were socialized to:

- *Be aggressive*
- *Be strong and powerful*
- *View problems as things to be fixed and to hold back emotions*
- *Devalue tenderness and vulnerability*
- *Be competitive*
- *Value what you do, as opposed to who you are*

As you consider the ways we have been socialized, keep in mind that varying degrees of adherence to male roles exist. Your family might have rejected many of them, so their impact on you could be minimal. No matter how you were raised, however, you have the opportunity to question them, especially as society as a whole is also questioning male and female roles. Once you determine how you've been influenced by socialization, you can then actively challenge these barriers to intimacy and remove them.

To Be Aggressive

As men, we were socialized to be aggressive in business and professional relationships. Aggression bleeds into relationships, and it doesn't bode well for intimacy with your partner. Aggression can heighten to the point where partners view conflict as win or lose. When one person wins, both partners lose out on feeling close.

Part of aggression is insisting that things go your way. There isn't much difference between aggression and control, both of which hinder intimacy. Let's say that your partner tells you he's uncomfortable when you talk on your cell phone while you drive. You disagree, and you tell him that he should drive his way and he should stop bringing it up. Fair enough, right? Not exactly, because you have just dismissed your partner's feelings. He's concerned about your reduced attention to driving while you're on the phone, so he must think that you are putting his safety at risk as well as yours. Every time you get in the car and decide to talk on the phone despite his protests, you have made the decision to dismiss his feelings again, provoking an argument in the process. If your partner is angry with you because he has asked you several times to stop the practice, he's not feeling good about you every time this comes up, you're not feeling good about him, and you both have to work at feeling close to each other again after an argument.

There are two other variations on this theme. To illustrate the first variation, let's say your partner tells you that he is uncomfortable with your being friends with your ex. You take an opposing stance in your mind yet don't voice your opinion. You outwardly agree to end the friendship but secretly make phone calls and send e-mails. When you aren't honest with your partner and don't come to an agreement you both feel comfortable with, you run the risk of resenting him. If you maintain contact with your ex after agreeing you won't just to get your partner off your back, you run another risk of getting caught. The situation could create feelings of guilt and cause you to try to justify your actions by picking fights, criticizing him, and getting defensive.

The second variation is to become passive-aggressive; that is, finding ways to get back at your partner for slights and hurts. To continue the example, let's say you agree to stop communicating with your ex. You comply with your partner's request, looking at it as a demand that you must agree to, and you stop all communication (the passive part). Over the next few months, you find yourself being less "in the mood" for sex. Or you stop picking up his dry cleaning, which you used to do regularly, and find excuses for not having the time. You're communicating your displeasure, but you're doing so indirectly (the aggressive part). Perhaps you're expecting him to figure out what you're doing and to approach you for a talk. Or perhaps you just want to punish him. Either way, intimacy is better maintained when you talk about your feelings directly than when you communicate them in passive-aggressive ways.

To Be Strong and Powerful

Being raised to believe that we must be strong, self-sufficient, and forceful inhibits intimacy. Take the need to be strong. Hiding the real you—who at times can be needy and dependent—means that you have created a façade. Showing your weaknesses is the real strength because you're risking vulnerability.

Let's say you feel the need to be completely independent. Are the following familiar? "I don't need to rely on anyone for anything" and "I can do it myself." A truly self-sufficient person can repair his car, program his computer, cook, clean, tend the garden, do odd jobs, and work full-time, which renders this kind of logic unreasonable. You were taught that, as a man, relying on others is okay for material needs, but wanting emotional support is considered needy. There's no difference between physical and emotional needs: The only true difference is that the first need is visible, the second is not.

When you the independent male feels dependent or needy, even for a short time, you're likely to become frightened. When you try to be tough and say you don't need anyone, you are simply refusing to acknowledge a real part of you. However, this is the antithesis of intimacy. You desire to be intimate, yet you back away. In fact, if your need for independence is very strong, you may be willing to risk your entire relationship rather than ask your partner for support.

Let's say that you feel insecure because your partner has gone back to school to get a degree, and he's spending a lot of time with his new school friends. You know he's not cheating on you, so you think you don't have a right to feel insecure or jealous, let alone to talk about it. So instead of bringing your feelings out into the open, you are sometimes a little distant and at other times quarrelsome. The distance and the fighting causes your partner to worry about what's going on, so he asks you whether everything is okay between you. You say yes. Overall, the deliberate attempts to distance yourself from him and have arguments causes you to feel bad about yourself, but you feel a strange sense of relief that he's fighting back and asking for reassurance. There's no way you're going to admit that you're feeling insecure and needy.

You can probably see where this scenario could lead. If the fighting and distance continue, one day your partner may realize that it's not about him. He may not know why you're doing it, but he will start to distance himself from you and stop engaging you when you start arguments. Over time, under the right circumstances, the bend in your relationship bond could break. The truth is that at times during your relationship, you will feel insecure and needy. For your relationship to survive, you need to accept these feelings and be prepared to reveal them to your partner as they arise. Otherwise, you may be putting your relationship at risk.

To View Problems As Needing to Be Fixed and to Hold Back Emotions

We were socialized to think that when there's a problem, we should fix it. However, many issues—those arising within the relationship and individually—can't be fixed but must be dealt with through a process of sharing feelings, listening, and achieving greater levels of acceptance.

For relationship issues, let's take the example of trust. Your partner has trouble trusting you because he has been burned in the past. In a real sense, the issue isn't personal. But it feels personal because it involves you. He recently listened to one of your voice-mail messages. You rightfully demand that he no longer listen to your voice-mail. Problem solved, right? Not really, because the main issue hasn't been addressed. Your partner needs to be able to share feelings that he finds scary because they make him feel vulnerable; and you need to be able to put your anger with the ostensible issue aside so that you set up an environment in which he feels safe to talk about it. One way is to start out by saying, "I see you're having trouble trusting me. Though I feel angry about it sometimes, I want to know why you'd feel this way" (whether you have done anything to violate his trust in the past or not). You're creating the space for him to open up to you about what's going on instead of focusing on "fixing" the voice-mail problem.

Regarding individual challenges, when your partner shares something with you and you immediately move into solution mode, you are making the assumption that your partner hasn't thought about what you're telling him, and it can come across as patronizing. If you are confident that he can solve his own problems, then relax and allow him to go through his own process of resolving them. As an example of an individual challenge, let's say your partner has lost his job and is depressed. Your reaction may be to try to find a solution so that he can get back on his feet. What if he doesn't bounce back? The process involves more than just being a cheerleader; it involves supplying emotional support and providing some gentle challenges along the way.

You would rightly ask, What about your own feelings? You may not feel entitled to certain emotions because they are not "rational." However, feelings follow their own logic, even when they don't appear to. What if your partner spends all his time looking for work and you feel jealous about the time he's spending away from you, even though you know it's irrational to feel this way?

In a relationship where you shift from quick fixes to living with process, it would be okay to talk about your frustration with his inability to find a job and your "irrational" feelings of jealousy. As you listen to how he feels, you will find he is equally frustrated, and he may be just as upset as you are about spending so much time apart. The shift in your dynamic is that you express your frustration with the situation along with him instead of blaming him for the situation.

Why is it important to share your feelings? You are already showing him your feelings by sighing when he can't find a misplaced item, changing the subject when he talks about his day, or getting annoyed over things that used to not bother you. Instead of sharing your true feelings, you act them out indirectly. By sharing them, you are telling him what is bothering you, a technique that can enhance intimacy.

Focusing on a solution also comes about when you have trouble feeling helpless. Men are socialized to be providers and leaders, so it's not uncommon to go into solution mode because we're threatened by our own feelings of helplessness and loss of control. So be aware the next time your partner comes to you with a problem. If you feel like jumping into solution mode, take a moment to reflect on what feelings are coming up for you. Be aware that the last thing he may need is advice, and you offer far greater assistance by being a witness to his difficulties, validating his feelings, and recognizing that he can solve his own problems.

Instead of offering a solution when your partner has a problem, you may be more helpful if you first get in touch with your own feelings of helplessness.

To Devalue Tenderness and Vulnerability

From the time we were small, we were taught indirectly to devalue feelings of tenderness and vulnerability. You may be hesitant to share these feelings because it exposes you to the possibility of embarrassment and ridicule. When you tell your partner how you feel, would he use it against you in the future? You may be reluctant to admit feeling needy or insecure as a result of your fears of being vulnerable.

Let's say that you're excited because your partner is coming home soon from a business trip. In the past when you spent time apart, you sent him a text message every day. At some point during the day, he would text you back. His current trip is coming to a close, and you text him with a sweet message and mention that you look forward to him coming home. He texts you back with a cold message: "Need to go to the office as soon as I get in. Won't be home till late."

Your initial feelings include being disappointed and hurt. You wonder whether it's worth bringing it up. But by then your feelings have subsided, so you tell yourself it's not worth saying anything until after he gets settled in. After a kiss hello and a cursory greeting, the next thing he says is "Where's the mail?" Now you're angry, but still you say nothing.

The next day, he sends you a warm text while you're both at work, and all seems to be forgotten until he sends you a brief e-mail later in the day that says, "Gotta work late again." There's no time estimate, no mention about what to do about dinner, and now you're livid.

Everything you "forgot" is back, and more.

Because you were socialized not to share your more vulnerable feelings, you feel hurt but say nothing, hoping that your feelings will change as he does. But if the change takes longer than you expect, either you start to treat him the same way he's treating you or you find yourself funneling your hurt feelings into anger. One day later in the week he walks in and you blast him for something small that is really in response to the sum total of how he's been treating you for the last several days. Your vulnerable feelings have been pushed aside in favor of showing him your anger. To increase closeness, instead of funneling your more vulnerable feelings into anger, talk them out. Ask him for reassurance that everything is okay, or tell him you're feeling hurt and disappointed.

One area where fear of vulnerability has a greater chance to play out is in regard to sex. The stereotypical role for men is to be ready to go anytime, anywhere. This myth puts an additional strain on intimacy. It isn't realistic to want sex every time your partner does. Sometimes, you simply may not be in the mood. If one of you has a higher libido, which is a usual occurrence, talk about it and try to work out a solution. It can be embarrassing to talk about masturbation as a way of meeting sexual needs, but being willing to talk about it means that this is one area of vulnerability that can be addressed.

To Be Competitive

Because men are socialized to get ahead through competition, we sometimes find ourselves being competitive with our partners. However, competition can lead to barriers against intimacy. Being competitive with your partner about who makes more money, who has the most friends, who is more concerned about the other person, better looking, smarter, and so on, inhibits intimacy because you lose the feeling of being on the same team and begin to feel more like enemies.

Part of the problem is that it's challenging to see where competition is playing out in your relationship. Couples can be competitive when it comes to addressing problems. To illustrate, let's say that part of your relationship pattern has been to show your anger by raising your voice. When you yell, he retaliates by giving you the Silent Treatment. One day, your partner sits you down to talk about the way you communicate. He begins by telling you that he gets upset when you yell at him, and he'd like you to tell him that you're angry with him rather than listen to you yell. You answer, "Why should I stop yelling? When you're angry with me, you give me the Silent Treatment, and you won't even admit you're angry with me. That's just as bad, maybe worse." Can you see how this response has an underlying competitive quality? The message is clear: You're admitting to a wrongdoing, but it's not as bad your partner's wrongdoing, so you're justified in continuing your behavior.

Another clue that you're being competitive is when you bait your partner. For example, if he gets angry and threatens to leave, you say, "Go ahead. What are you waiting for? See if I care." Not only are you hiding a more vulnerable feeling of fear, you are creating an air of one-upmanship.

The remedy for competition is cooperation. Learning to cooperate rather than compete is crucial to intimacy. When you're in a situation akin to those just mentioned, expand your perspective of seeing only your side. When your partner approaches you with a problem, try not to one-up him or counter him with something he has done to you, even if it's exactly the same thing. Instead, consider how you are contributing to the situation. As you do, you are becoming more cooperative.

To Value What You Do, As Opposed to Who You Are

As men, we were socialized to emphasize the importance of what we *do* as opposed to who we *are*. What men primarily "do" is work for a living, and success is judged by the amount of money you make or the objects you accumulate. Although you naturally want to feel productive through your endeavors, you are socialized to feel that if you don't make a certain amount of money or have a certain amount of prestige, you don't have value. Similar to what the character George Bailey learned in the movie *It's a Wonderful Life,* material success at all costs brings emptiness, whereas relationships and friendships are what bring joy and satisfaction.

Questioning What It Means to Be a Man

As a gay man, you have had to question society's beliefs about what it means to be gay. Your questioning may have begun as you explored your family of origin's religious beliefs, or the myths they passed on about gay people. This should lead to questioning other beliefs, including what it means to be a man and how men are supposed to behave in a relationship. For men who do not adhere to traditional roles, sustained intimacy—which includes allowing yourself to be vulnerable, interdependent, and cooperative—comes more naturally.

By taking the one-down position—giving up power for the sake of intimacy—you send a message that you care about your partner and the relationship, and you are showing a high degree of vulnerability. You are saying to your partner that you are willing to sacrifice something to achieve something else that is more meaningful and mutually beneficial.

When you and your partner don't ascribe to what it means to be "male," you are able to cry in front of each other without feeling ashamed. With the walls down, you allow yourselves to be more vulnerable, which leads to greater intimacy. You are also more flexible. Flexibility is an essential aspect of cooperation and is a building block for intimacy. When you're not locked into the "male" role, you have the opportunity to recognize the power differences in your relationship and to talk about them in a productive way. As a result, you and your partner can equalize the differences so that you both feel comfortable about where you live, the activities you pursue, the restaurants you frequent, and mutual friends. In other words, you are better able to negotiate your everyday living together.

Putting It Together

By virtue of being a male couple, you must deal with continuing societal pressures and varying degrees of support from your families of origin. You and your partner get closer by resolving these challenges and drawing on the strengths that arise as a result of working together to overcome them. Furthermore, by questioning what you were taught about what it means to be a man and to be gay, intimacy is within reach.

We next focus on how to deal with relationship difficulties that usually don't emerge until well after your relationship begins. They include financial instability, life transition, lack of cooperation, and drifting apart.

CHAPTER 10

Challenges over Time

SOME CHALLENGES DON'T emerge until several years into your relationship. They often result in barriers to intimacy and can be challenging to resolve. However, with patience, cooperation, and willingness to put forth effort, they can make the bond of your relationship stronger as you attempt to work through them.

Major Challenges

As the years of your relationship progress, several major challenges may emerge. They include:

- *Financially irresponsible partners*
- *Life transitions*
- *Negotiating sexual limits*
- *The presence of a sexually transmitted disease*
- *Lack of cooperation*
- *Drifting apart*

Financially Irresponsible Partners

People with financial problems tend to fall on a continuum. On one end, people have a decent income and set aside money for retirement, but they worry about their future. Toward the middle, someone can be in good financial shape but have something happen that gives him a major jolt, such as being laid off, having a major car repair, or experiencing a medical emergency. If something happens to your partner to challenge his financial situation, then being supportive becomes important to help him through the situation. The roles may switch someday, and hopefully he will be there for you during a difficult stretch.

Let's say that you are fairly responsible financially. You have never been late for credit card or car loan payments, you balance your checkbook, and you regularly put aside money for retirement. Your partner, on the other hand, has not been so fastidious. His credit card payments have sometimes been late, and a couple of times he forgot to make a loan payment, so his credit history is so-so. Even though he makes decent money, he seldom has enough to go on nice vacations or to take you out. Furthermore, he cares about his future but hasn't started saving for retirement.

After living together, it wouldn't be unusual for you and your partner to argue about money. Your partner may claim that his financial life doesn't affect you, but you believe it does. To prove your point, you remind your partner that you don't go to certain places unless *you* pay, and perhaps you've had to lend your partner money a few times.

If you approach the situation emphasizing concern for your partner rather than your own aggravation, there's a better chance of having your partner admit he could do better. He might even ask you for help. You can keep separate bank accounts and pool some of your money into a joint account for household expenses. You could agree on a split on household expenses and bills that isn't necessarily fifty-fifty but is comfortable for both of you. You could ask your partner to cut up his credit cards or turn over his paychecks. As these possibilities illustrate, you learn to accept your differences as your financial skill becomes your partner's gain.

On the far end of the continuum, some people are financially unstable and irresponsible. If you enter into a relationship with someone like this, you may not be aware of the extent of your partner's problems with money. He takes you to dinner, has a decent place, nice furniture, and a good car, so you think his financial picture is bright. However, the outward picture isn't an accurate reflection of how he's doing. He may have gone deeply into debt to pay for everything.

Whether he has the trappings of success or not, your partner's financial situation may be bleak. Defaulting on school loans, failing to keep up with credit card payments, and needing to pay back money loaned by friends or family all point to financial instability.

Maybe his financial situation wasn't horrible when you first got together but has steadily deteriorated. Sometimes, a history of financial instability is an indication of emotional problems. Signs include your partner's having a history of defaulting on loans or credit cards, being fired or leaving jobs, or losing friendships because of money. His problems may stem from immaturity, old emotional wounds, or a high degree of internalized homophobia that leads to feeling worthless.

Perhaps you didn't see it coming when you first got together. You may have overlooked some of the warning signs; and you may have justified going forward because of his positive qualities, or perhaps you entertained the possibility of helping him (the rescuer-wounded bird dynamic).

Because you initially accepted his explanations and excuses about his financial woes, it takes time (and more situations) to realize that his reasons are just excuses, such as telling you it's only temporary or that he's had some bad breaks. Your coming to terms with his situation is first a process of accepting that he has a problem. Once you do, because his financial situation will remain the way it is, it's time to take care of yourself.

Coping with a Financially Unstable Partner

The worst-case scenario is having financial ties, such as owning a home together, keeping a joint checking account, loaning him money and not being repaid, or sharing credit cards with a partner who is on the unstable end of the continuum. If you're in any of these situations, take some steps to protect yourself. Loosen your financial ties by establishing a separate bank account. If you already have your own account, you can still keep a joint account for household expenses. To prevent future overdraft notices, call the bank or go online regularly to get the balance and ask your partner to hand over the joint checks and debit cards. His refusal gives you more reason to establish your own account and shut down the joint account if necessary.

Put loans to him in writing. You may want to solicit the help of a professional to draft the proper wording. If your partner objects or says it's because you don't trust him, ignore his protests and remind him that you now have two types of relationships—partner and lender—and the best thing to do is to keep the two relationships separate. If he refuses to sign it, then you have the information you need to take further steps to protect yourself and your assets.

Co-owning a house or other property may mean soliciting the advice of a lawyer, but the major point is to take care of yourself. This is a time when it's more crucial to put your needs above your partner's needs, unless you don't want to prevent yourself from falling into a black hole with him. Once you take steps to protect your assets, you will start to feel better because you will be taking some of your (self) control back. At the same time, it will help your partner. He can only learn the consequences of his actions and have the opportunity to change course once you no longer bail him out. The situation isn't always hopeless. Creative thinking, combined with time, can lead to unique solutions.

Life Transitions

As a couple, you will go through periods when one partner experiences a major change, such as the death of a friend or parent, loss of a job, or the birth of a child. A change in circumstances can create uncertainty, especially when the relationship is new. Consider how you would react to the following situation. Let's say that you've been with your partner for a few years. One day, your partner tells you that he has an opportunity for a promotion—in another city. What would you do if you really like where you live, enjoy your job, and value your friendships? How would the two of you proceed?

There's no one answer to this question, but it's important to talk about it with your partner, sleep on it, and talk some more. It's okay to lose sleep over it, argue about what to do, and come back to discuss it again. It's just as important to start from the premise that you have two sets of needs, two perspectives, and essentially three options for proceeding.

The first option is that you stay. Does your partner have other options for moving up, such as switching jobs to another company locally, or would he have to relocate to progress in his career? Does he lack a college education, which makes advancing more difficult if he moves to another company? If he stays because you adamantly don't want to move, you are possibly setting yourselves up for him to resent you later on.

The second option is to move. But what happens when you don't want to leave your job or the city you live in? In addition to looking at the questions above, how easy would it be for you to get a job in another city? Do your (possibly aging) parents live in your town or city? Would they have sufficient help if you moved? What about your close friends? Do they still live in your city or have many of them moved? If you both move because he insists upon it, you're possibly setting yourself up to regret your decision and, in turn, to blame him for it.

The third option, which some couples can work through, is for him to move and you to stay. Although possibly the diciest choice in the short-term, it may keep your relationship intact for the long-term. It could prevent one of you from resenting the other one to the point where one of you could undermine the relationship. Some couples do manage to continue their relationships while living in different cities. Although long-distance relationships have their own set of challenges, you may have to give this option serious consideration, at least for a trial period. If he moves, you can always move later, or he can come back after you realize that you can't live in separate cities. Perhaps it won't work out for him and he will want to move back. On the other hand, if it's a temporary relocation—a year or two—see one another as often as possible until your situations change and it's possible to be in the same city again.

Negotiating Sexual Limits

If you and your partner have opted for monogamy, you don't need to negotiate anything. But what if your feelings are changing? You may have started off as monogamous, but made other decisions as the years went by. To make matters more complicated, with the shifting definition of sex, especially with the Internet and other forms of technology, the lines between monogamy and non-monogamy have blurred.

You may find yourself tempted to have sex outside your relationship and to find reasons not to tell your partner, which includes fear of the daunting possibility of a future discussion of non-monogamy. You may think you can be trusted because *you* know that having sex with other men won't lead to your leaving him. Or you convince yourself to believe that telling him would devastate him, so you don't.

These rationalizations may be covering up a fear that he will leave you. However, cheating on your partner is destructive to intimacy. When you cheat, you automatically feel the need to lie or to cover up, even when he asks you what you did the day before or whom you had lunch with. As a result, the guilt you're feeling will come out in indirect ways and affect the relationship. To justify having sex outside the relationship in your own mind, you may start an argument or find other ways to distance yourself from him. You might become extra nice to assuage your guilt. You may even take the offensive position by accusing him or assuming he's having sex with other guys, which again is an attempt to justify your actions.

Before you step outside the relationship, gather the courage to talk to your partner about wanting to have sex with others. In fact, talking about your desires may *reduce* the urge to have outside sex or help you to come up with solutions that don't include sex with other men. Your partner may be having similar fantasies, and you can talk about options. To think about negotiating sex outside the relationship, let's look at Roberto and David's challenge.

CASSE STUDY: *Roberto and David*

Roberto and David have settled into their relationship. For a long time, Roberto did some soul searching about why his last relationship didn't work out. He realized that most of the problem related to sex and trust. He demanded that his ex trust him, but he didn't feel worthy of his trust. Roberto cheated and justified his actions by believing it didn't affect the love he had for him. His ex distrusted him and accused him of cheating. Instead of admitting to it, Roberto turned on him. He got angry and he hurt him at every opportunity. When his ex started retaliating, Roberto felt even more justified in having an affair.

When his relationship with David began, Roberto was determined to stay monogamous. About a year ago, after David's mother died, David became filled with grief and gained a lot of weight. More and more, Roberto is having sexual fantasies about other men, and he finds himself increasingly turned off by David's weight and equally troubled by his own fantasies.

Roberto has been placing himself in increasingly risky situations. He had come close to having sex with someone last month, although he knows he could destroy what he has with David by secretly having sex outside the relationship. With encouragement from a good friend, he gathers the courage to approach David with the truth.

One day, Roberto tells David that he wants to talk to him about something important. The two of them sit in the living room as Roberto begins. "You know, David, I love you so much. I want to be with you for the rest of my life." David nods slowly as Roberto continues, "I know how hard this last year has been for you. I don't know what it's like to lose a parent, but it's got to be horrible, and I understand why you're depressed. I want to do everything I can to continue to support you in any way I can." David nods again because Roberto has been very supportive for the last year, and his words ring true.

"As much as I want to be faithful, I am getting sexually frustrated. We hardly have sex anymore, and jerking off isn't doing it for me. I'm not as attracted to you since you gained weight and between that and you not wanting to have sex, I'm having fantasies about other men. I don't like feeling this way, but I'm at my wits end. I don't mean this to be a threat. I have been honest with you from day one, and I can tell you I have not had sex outside the relationship. I'll hang in there for as long as I can. But I need to start meeting my sexual needs."

David cries, and Roberto holds him. When he finishes crying, he looks at Roberto and says, "Since my mom died, I don't know. I just shut down. I knew that one day you would come to me with this. Who can blame you? I want to look good and I want to have sex with you, but I just can't. Not right now. I'm only thirty-three and I lost my mom, and it's so unfair. I'm too young and I can't deal with it. You have been fantastic this past year. I don't want you to have sex with other guys. Let me talk to my psychiatrist about my medication, which has lowered my drive. Maybe he can change my meds or add something. I can try to lose some weight. Give me a few months, and if that doesn't work, we can look at other options, including letting you have sex with other guys. But if you do, we'll have to talk about some rules."

The Rules

Gay men who have sex outside of their relationships don't necessarily have completely open relationships. A totally open relationship means that a couple places no restrictions on whom each partner has sex with or when. A person in an open relationship doesn't need to consult his partner; he can mention his sexual exploits or not, depending on the situation and on what each partner wants to know at the time.

Open relationships work for some couples. They enjoy sexual adventures together or separately. Many of these couples continue to have sex with each other, but some have sex only with others. Some couples go to bathhouses and bookstores together, or separately, and they get off on discussing their adventures.

You may not wish to have this degree of openness. If so, "the rules" are guidelines you agree to when either of you has sex with others. You can both place some restrictions on when to have sex, where it takes place, and with whom. This is done to increase each person's comfort level and limit the possibility that outside sex will turn into a threat to the relationship. For example, you may agree to restrict yourselves to three-ways when you are both on vacation. You could restrict outside sex to places away from your home or neighborhood altogether. The no-call-back rule limits you to anonymous sex and prohibits you from providing contact information so that you don't see the same person twice. If the no-call-back rule is too restrictive, you may choose not to impose this restriction and allow for alternatives. No matter how solid the relationship is, however, couples run a greater risk when they allow outside relationships than when they restrict themselves to anonymous sex.

You may want to establish constraints on the type of sex you and your partner have outside the relationship. For example, you may prefer to limit outside sex to mutual masturbation. Once you decide to be with others, it's okay to require the use of condoms when you have sex with others. If you want to increase safety, add condoms to sex with your partner, regardless of what the two of you decide concerning sex with others. It's not that either one of you might violate the rules. Rather, it's about comfort and knowing that there's a possibility, albeit slight, that something could go wrong with the protection between you or him and an outside person.

You may prefer to know about his sexual exploits and have him talk about them. You do not need to have the same rule if one of you enjoys hearing about it but the other does not. Alternatively, you may prefer a don't-ask-don't-tell rule whereby sex outside the relationship is not talked about, either generally or specifically, but it is mutually agreed upon and understood.

In another variation, let's say you started out as a non-monogamous couple but you agree to close the relationship well into it. If you have a relationship that allows for outside sex, talk to your partner about wanting to be monogamous. Many couples make the transition from non-monogamy to monogamy after being together a while.

Regardless of what you agree to, cheating occurs when one partner violates the rules. Before you suspect that your partner has strayed past a sexual boundary, initiate an occasional conversation to see how it's going. If you have violated a rule, tell him as soon as possible so that your guilt or his suspicions don't start to have a negative impact on intimacy.

Whether or not you and your partner allow outside sexual activities, the Internet is blurring the line between monogamy and non-monogamy. Where do you draw the line? Is it when you watch guys jacking off on a live Web site? When you're in a chat room? What if you start corresponding with someone and the conversation turns sexual? What would you call swapping pictures with him?

The Internet and the changing definition of sex have blurred the lines of monogamy.

The Internet is not the only place where the lines become hazy. What about going for a massage and the therapist offers a happy ending? Would it matter if the therapist was naked or if full body contact occurred during the massage?

The point to asking these questions is to help you determine what is acceptable to both of you in these gray areas. One rule of thumb is that when you won't talk to your partner about something you're doing, you are probably cheating. If so, reconsider your actions and think about talking to your partner.

The Presence of a Sexually Transmitted Disease

A sexually transmitted disease (STD) can come up in your relationship in one of three ways. The first way is for one partner to have a disease (such as hepatitis, herpes, or HIV) prior to starting the relationship. The person with the disease reveals this to the other. The second way is for a partner to have it but be unaware of it until after a relationship has begun; both partners learn about a preexisting STD at the same time. The third way is for a partner to acquire it during the relationship.

The presence of an STD can put a lot of pressure on a relationship. The person who has it may be scared of infecting his partner, and the other partner may be equally scared of contracting it. The uninfected partner may suffer from being a "worried-well" person. This can lead to less fulfilling sex, or a lack of it, in the relationship. If the uninfected person is worried-well, outside intervention may help you work through an issue of this magnitude. Several discussions can help, and you should try to negotiate safety while having as fulfilling a sex life as possible.

Sex isn't the only place where challenges develop. Let's say your partner learns he is HIV-positive while you are together. He may start to concentrate on his health and have less energy for the relationship. He may join a support group, spend more time at the gym, and find other ways to improve his health. Meanwhile, you may start to feel left out and even insecure about the newly found focus on himself, the new people he meets, and the recently added activities. At the same time, he may take medications that have harmful side effects. You may begin to feel helpless about being unable to take away his suffering. It makes sense that your feelings and needs would take a back seat, but at some point intimacy can wane if your feelings build up and you don't talk about them.

A more serious rift may develop if your partner contracted an STD after your relationship began. The problem that's going to arise is lack of trust and a feeling of betrayal. This makes it even more important for you to make a determined effort at increased communication. Look for the opportunity to express your feelings about what happened. You may need some time to think about what you want to do, and you have the right to take some time for yourself.

If you are the person who has the STD, you may think that your partner doesn't understand what you're going through. His lack of understanding can lead to frustration and resentment. You may see him turning to his friends for more outside support, which can also lead to feelings of insecurity. Both of you may begin to feel intimacy slipping away.

When you don't feel justified in your feelings, fight the temptation to say nothing. Give voice to your emotions, in spite of wanting to defer to your partner. This doesn't mean you should frequently complain or make unreasonable demands on him, but intimacy needs room for your feelings. At the same time, temper them by showing him empathy.

Work on solutions together. For example, if you are HIV-negative and your partner is positive, become invested in his health by taking him to the gym, going for walks, and buying healthy food. Ask him to go with you to a support group for sero-discordant couples, or suggest couples counseling. By becoming enrolled, your feelings of closeness may increase. You are more likely to stay connected if you view this as a relationship challenge. Likewise, if you are the one with HIV, let your partner know you are trying to understand what he's going through and encourage discussions on how you can assist each other. Take a team approach and support each other through these times. Intimacy will expand as a result.

Even though the course of HIV has changed with the advent of life-extending medications, issues related to mortality will naturally arise. He may react to his seroconversion by re-doubling his efforts to be healthy. But he might use unhealthy coping strategies, such as drugs, alcohol, or other addictive activities. Be careful not to enable him to use these strategies by making excuses for him, thinking it will go away, or doing it with him. By taking care of yourself, you are also taking care of him. You may be creating a rift in the short-run, but you're giving him the opportunity to come around to make better choices.

Lack of Cooperation

Cooperation is essential for sustaining intimacy. When you both cooperate, each of you feels respected and heard even when you don't agree. Losing the spirit of cooperation, however, can lead to an every-man-for-himself attitude.

Although couples never have an equal investment toward cooperating, each of you should commit to getting along. If he doesn't want to cooperate with you because he isn't invested, there's something seriously wrong, and the sooner you take action, the better. Part of the problem is that taking action would be making waves. Risks are involved, and these include a widening rift. If you learn that he has completely divested and that you are doing all the work to keep it together, making waves at least gives intimacy a chance to be restored. When you ask him to go with you to couples counseling, for example, his agreement will probably signify whether he is committed to cooperating. If he goes, it's a sign that he may start cooperating with you because he has enough of an investment to work on the relationship.

Ironically, if you are the caretaker in a caretaker-carefree relationship dynamic, your attempts to change him will only solidify the dynamic. You might be the one who brings up issues and wants to work on them, and he says no because to him everything is "fine;" if this happens, you run the risk of his losing respect for you or seeing you as nagging. Consequently, you will feel frustrated because he never listens to you. If he rolls his eyes or belittles you, he isn't listening. As time goes on, his lack of regard for you could become more blatant. Your efforts to make him respond differently to you may work for a while. But before long, he will go back to the way he was. This can lead to your feeling exasperated and helpless.

Start taking care of yourself more than you used to. Go into individual therapy should he refuse to go with you for couples counseling. If you have been subjugating your needs, be more self-centered and work on taking your power back. This translates into action by soliciting the support of friends and family, spending time with them, focusing your energies on your own personal growth, and not shying away from conflict.

Drifting Apart

As I noted in chapter 5, you and your partner probably went through a period of shifting away from exclusively focusing on each other to including other people and interests. This process is a natural shift, and as the dynamics change and as each person adjusts accordingly, relationship harmony is maintained. However, a potential threat to intimacy arises when either of you (or both) takes independence too far. The bond can start to fray and you don't feel as connected as you used to feel. You develop your own interests as he develops his, and you're not making each other aware of how you're growing and changing. This shift takes place at the expense of intimacy because you are both not keeping each other informed of what's happening.

Growing apart can be more than just not keeping each other informed. When you spend significant time away from each other, you won't feel a genuine connection. You and your partner may end up spending more time with friends. Perhaps you are tempted to have an affair because he's not meeting your needs; likewise, you realize you wouldn't mind if he has an affair.

So you have come to the realization that you have drifted apart to the point where you feel like strangers living in the same household. More often than not, growing apart and not caring is a substitute for increasing emotional distance resulting from relationship dissatisfaction, ongoing problems, and escalating feelings of resentment, hurt, and anger toward each other. Instead of approaching the issues head on, you and your partner are feigning indifference, which becomes a cover-up for anguish and distress. As the process continues, threats to intimacy increase. You may become increasingly dissatisfied with the relationship and have thoughts of leaving. You grow steadily dissatisfied and don't inform him you are entertaining the thought of ending the relationship.

Relationship Escapes

You may attempt to cope with your dissatisfaction and avoid facing your challenges by having an affair or anonymous sex. These are ways for you to seek out the intimacy you're not getting with your partner. It's also an example of a relationship escape, which is a way of leaving the relationship without ending it.

Other relationship escapes make it easier for you to cope with a lack of intimacy. These escapes include alcohol and drugs, food, gambling, the Internet, and work. By finding these ways to cope with your dissatisfaction, you allow yourself to feel bad about the relationship but not motivated enough to take action. You are easing the pressure to confront your relationship challenges.

Closing the escape hatches

When you put an end to escaping, you are essentially going to feel worse. The pressure to make changes intensifies because you have no pressure valve. You're giving yourself the opportunity to do something. Your major task is to reestablish closeness. Your relationship may need to be shaken up, which means going to couples counseling, hiring a relationship coach, or going to a couples workshop.

Stopping your escapes is no easy task. For example, let's say you have fantasies you indulge in on the Internet. How can you simply stop getting on the Internet, especially because you know that the unhappiness you're feeling about your relationship will only intensify? One answer lies in taking a "short-term pain, long-term gain" approach. The short-term relief you feel when you escape is only placing a Band-Aid on a large wound. It doesn't make the problems disappear, so the pain is still with you. By stopping, you place *more* pressure on yourself to confront your relationship challenges so that you have the opportunity to work through them and to restore intimacy.

In the meantime, because you can only control your actions, focus on redirecting your energies back to the relationship. If you're not having sex with your partner, the first step isn't necessarily initiating it. Rather, you may want to initiate nonsexual touch: a little back rub, a hug, or a sympathetic touch on the arm when he tells you about something that upset him during his day. To reestablish a physical connection, initiate a more intimate touch, such as holding him while you are lying naked in bed. You don't need to turn it into sex—yet. Rather, keep increasing closeness. Sex will happen more naturally as a result of better feelings toward one another.

Think about ways to increase intimacy. When you have problems you want to address, consider putting them on the shelf as you focus on getting reacquainted with him, going out to dinner or on other kinds of dates, and reopening the lines of communication. Confronting him with issue after issue can work against you by creating more conflict. You have plenty of time to discuss issues, but you will have more productive discussions once you have reestablished a sense of connection.

Let's say you are trying to bring back a feeling of intimacy and have made several unsuccessful attempts to have sex. Keep in mind that the way you treat him when you're not in the bedroom is going to influence his desire to have sex with you. Immediately turning your nonexistent sex life into an issue may actually move you away from your goal because it puts pressure on your partner. Before you take any action, ask yourself whether it's going to move you toward or away from your goal of reestablishing intimacy. As you become consistent in being calm, respectful, and a good listener, you are increasing your chances to reestablish your sex life.

This process of restoring intimacy can be a slow and, at times, tedious. As you start to feel close again, issues that led to drifting apart are going to come into focus. Once you have begun to reestablish a sense of closeness, attempt to open up communication about the issues. Try to learn about and understand the problems he is having with you. Be receptive and listen to his issues with an open mind; that way, there is a better chance he will give you the same consideration.

As you open up discussions on long-standing issues, you risk upsetting the status quo. What can seem to be a setback (arguing, expressing long-held emotions) is actually moving forward. Beneath the veneer of indifference lies hurt and anger. Reconciliation will not be a straight road, but rather one with twists and turns.

When you are drifting apart or not cooperating with each other, first try to work at reestablishing intimacy on your own (as a couple). Should that not work, enlist the aid of a couples counselor to help you interrupt your pattern of relating to each other. You want interruption because it gives you the opportunity to shift your dynamics. There are many other reasons why seeing a couples counselor can be helpful, the most important being that each of you takes responsibility for your part of the problem and gets to the real reasons for drifting apart.

Putting It Together

Many demanding challenges don't emerge until well into your relationship, and neither you nor your partner could have predicted them. You may find yourselves troubled by financial instability, unexpected life transitions, sexual concerns, uncooperativeness, and drifting apart. As you gain the courage to talk about them with your partner, you can successfully resolve these challenges and grow closer to your partner.

However, these and other obstacles to intimacy may be related to greater troubles. The focus of the next chapter is on the considerable difficulties arising from drug use, relationship violence, and mental illness.

CHAPTER 11
The Biggest Threats

SOME BARRIERS TO intimacy seem so insurmountable that you may be thinking about ending the relationship. Even though you think you may be out of options, there are ways to deal with serious problems and for the relationship to survive. Whether it's substance abuse, relationship violence, or mental illness, ordinarily the focus initially needs to be on each individual. Once you confront these issues individually, you can address them as a couple.

Substance Abuse and Addictions

Perhaps you drink or get high with your partner. What happens if you notice that you stop at a certain point but he keeps going till he passes out? What if he is staying out late with his friends and comes home wasted? What should you do if you find some paraphernalia after he tells you that he's stopped using?

Why It's Difficult to Come to Terms with Substance Abuse

When it comes to substance abuse, the key word here is shame. Users feel bad about their addictions, and their partners feel bad for tolerating or encouraging their use. This gives rise to several unhelpful coping strategies that both partners use to avoid facing the fact that a substance is coming between you and your partner. One coping strategy is denial, which is a defense against accepting something that will ultimately prove to be painful. Other coping strategies include rationalizing and minimizing the problem. Rationalizing happens when you find reasons for your partner's drinking. Perhaps he's out of a job or depressed about losing a friend or family member. He is likely to find reasons for drinking or drugging to excess, which would only serve to reinforce ideas you have about his use. Minimizing includes thinking that he uses it only on the weekends, or that as long as he keeps his job, he's okay.

Furthermore, some relationship dynamics include a history of growing up in a family where you have developed the role of go-between or caretaker. Perhaps one or both parents were addicted to a substance, and you had to take care of your siblings. Although growing up in an addictive household can lead more easily to your developing the role of caretaker, that role could have been conferred upon you by a nonaddictive household as well. Perhaps you were the only male or were the oldest, or you displayed an early propensity for taking care of others.

Regardless, protecting your partner is known as enabling, and it is a major characteristic when caretaking becomes codependency. Codependence includes meeting certain needs by having an addicted partner. Possible needs include the need to be needed, the need for drama (as evidenced by repeated rescue attempts), and the need to focus on some else's problems rather than one's own. To avoid being abandoned, the codependent person will do anything to hang on to a relationship with an addict, including accepting scraps of approval from the addict while watching his own sense of self-worth plummet.

It is not shameful to come to terms with an addiction. Science has brought us to the point where we can understand the brain chemistry involved in addiction. However, society's beliefs, such as assertions that addictions stem from weakness or lack of moral character, make it more challenging.

Crystal Meth

In addition to working as a psychotherapist, at one time I oversaw a clinic that treated gay men addicted to crystal meth. Crystal deserves special consideration partly because it has become popular and partly because gay men sometimes include it in the category of such party drugs as GHB, Special K, and Ecstasy. But crystal is highly addictive, closely associated with sexual compulsivity, and it creates a dual addiction. It is a large factor in the demise of many gay male relationships.

Without going into details about all the properties or effects of crystal, I'd like to mention that crystal creates a false sense of intimacy. You can have amazing sexual experiences with your partner (and others), but it doesn't take long for crystal to get hold of you. Talk to any crystal meth addict and he will almost certainly tell you that it has destroyed, or nearly destroyed, his relationship, that he has done things sexually he *never* thought he would do, and that he is mortified at the thought of some of his activities. The following scenario between Jason and Gregory highlights another problem.

CASE STUDY: *Jason and Gregory*

Recall that Jason and Gregory made plans to have a party. The night of the party, one of their friends, Ross, brings crystal with him. Ross knows that Jason is in recovery, but Ross is relapsing and is in the midst of a three-day "run," so he doesn't care about anything except getting high. At one point, Jason takes a guest's coat to the back bedroom, and Ross follows him. Before Jason can think, Ross takes out some crystal, snorts it, and places the rest in front of Jason. Just then, Gregory walks in with another coat. He bats Ross's hand away from Jason and demands that Ross leave. Wanting to avoid a scene, Ross quickly exits.

Gregory, shaking with anger, demands to know whether Jason had already taken some, because if so, he's going to tell everyone to go home. Jason vehemently denies it; with a wary eye, Gregory says that if he notices anything funny about Jason's behavior, he will tell everyone to leave. He also says they will talk after the party.

Dealing with a Partner Who Is Addicted to Substances

When substances are being abused by your partner, you have a third partner in your relationship. This third partner is going to make intimacy more difficult, even though episodes of drama, followed by periods of intense reconciliation, *feel* like intimacy. Rather, they are part of an unhealthy cycle that exacts a larger and larger cost.

You have many ways to remove yourself from the dramatic cycle of living with an addict. The first place to start is to admit that you cannot make him stop using drugs or alcohol, and that you cannot stop him from going on a downward spiral. This is why I view addiction as an individual issue. You can take some actions as a couple once he decides to get clean, but he must come to the conclusion on his own that he's an addict and go through the process of getting clean because he decides to do so.

Where does this leave you? You must take care of yourself. Part of self-care is to stop making excuses for him, not only to yourself but also to friends and family. Try to stop taking care of him when he is too hung over or drunk to do something that he committed to do. Try not to shield him from any consequences, including legal or financial.

If it's too difficult to let him face the consequences, at least lessen the impact his actions have on you. At the same time, bolster your support system. This is one time to open up to your family and friends (not his) about the problem. If you've been shutting people out because of the "secret," let them in. It's important to come out of this closet and not let shame get in the way of relying on your support system.

At the same time you let go of insisting that he go to rehab or a twelve-step program, consider going to Alanon (a twelve-step group for the family members of an addict) or a nonspiritual alternative such as Save Ourselves or Rational Recovery. When you no longer accept his excuses, lies, or deceit, and you start to stand on your own, he will have to look at himself through a different lens. He may get the help he needs and he may not. In the meantime, you are taking extraordinary steps to take care of yourself.

It's fairly strong to say that your addicted partner is lying and deceitful, but both are part of the disease of addiction. For him to survive emotionally, he needs to lie to other people about what he's doing. Even if he admits to using substances, he will underestimate the quantity he uses or how often he does them, and he will minimize how much his drug use affects the relationship and his life. Therefore, lying, in addition to rationalizing, becomes a coping strategy that allows him to continue using.

Part of taking care of yourself, which may be the "final straw" strategy, is to give him ultimatums you intend to keep. One option is to tell him that if he gets drunk at a get-together, you will leave him there and he will have to take a cab. Likewise, tell him you're going to stop paying his bills.

Keep your promises. He will learn to respect your word. Where this is leading to is giving him the ultimate choice. Once he has started believing you, give him a choice between you and the substances. This may be the motivation he needs to get help. You need to be emotionally and financially prepared to keep your final promise once you have given him the ultimatum.

Let's say your partner gets sober. Although this is going to solve a lot of old problems, new ones come about. You may learn that without your enabling role, you are missing something in the relationship. You may discover why you enabled him for so long. Additionally, many of the old problems will not be solved by his going into recovery, and you may have developed some false expectations about what stopping substance abuse will do for the relationship. To the contrary, his sobriety may uncover serious new issues that you and your partner will have to deal with. You both may have to devote some of your energies toward yourselves instead of into the relationship, so intimacy is likely to be sacrificed for some time.

If you are with someone who is in recovery, it is important to learn about the disease and be prepared for what you would do if he has a relapse. In the illustration above regarding Jason and Gregory, notice that Gregory said that he will keep watch on Jason's behavior and call off the party if he notices that his behavior is strange. Gregory made a promise to himself that he would have no part of Jason's drug use; and though he hasn't relapsed thus far, Gregory knows it could happen at any time, and that he will need to take care of himself if he does relapse. Ironically, Gregory's self-care helps Jason feel safer. By drawing a very rigid line, Jason knows that if he crosses it just once, there will be consequences. These consequences are part of what keeps Jason from doing drugs when he feels he's at risk for using.

Mental Illness

Just about everyone gets depressed, has moments of anxiety, has ups and downs, and can feel distracted. These states should not be confused with clinical depression, anxiety disorders, bipolar disorder, or ADHD (attention deficit and hyperactivity disorder). Once you have learned that your partner has a mental illness, take steps to familiarize yourself with it, understand what he's going through, and support him to the best of your ability.

There are many Web sites for people suffering from mental illness and their family members. By familiarizing yourself with his condition and trying to understand what he's going through, support him as best you can while you brace yourself for the next episode or problem related to his illness. Some disorders are relatively easy to treat, but others start at a very early age and become part of a person's basic personality. These problems, known as personality disorders, are very resistant to change. Rather than being pessimistic, adjust to his condition. Once he becomes aware of his diagnosis, you have even more cause for optimism.

Coping with a Partner Who Is Mentally Ill

It's difficult to deal with a partner who has a mental illness. You might be using the coping strategies you would adopt if you were dealing with an addict—denial, rationalization, and minimizing the extent of problem. However, if your partner is severely depressed, it is impossible not to be affected, especially if he suffers from what is known as an "angry depression." He cannot contain his pain and anger, and he will take it out on you.

Once your partner is aware of what's wrong with him and is taking steps to get better, trust him to know what he ought to do. Usually, he will want to enlist your support and that of his friends, a therapist, and a psychiatrist. Because you are part of his support system, be empathetic. Listen to him when he's down and avoid giving advice or judging him. Try your best to understand what he's going through.

It's difficult to find a balance between supporting your partner and taking care of yourself, but it's important to try. Supplement your attention to him with self-care. Solicit the support of your friends and family, groups you belong to, and, if need be, a therapist. Don't hesitate to find a therapist if you feel helpless or stressed out. Should your partner refuse treatment, seek therapy for your own peace of mind. Whether he goes or not, you have the opportunity to learn ways to deal with his specific problems in the least detrimental ways to you and the relationship.

Relationship Violence

The extent of verbal and physical violence among gay partners hasn't been documented until recently, and it is fairly consistent with rates among heterosexuals. Two types of violence exist in relationships: Common couple violence (coined by the author Michael Johnson) and domestic violence. These two types of violence have major differences and therefore should be approached accordingly. With common couple violence, fights can get physical, and the combat is mutual. One key feature of common couple violence is that neither partner is afraid of the other. On the other hand, with domestic violence, one partner is very afraid of the other. Domestic violence usually increases over time and becomes more severe. With domestic violence, when the victim defends himself and fights back, it's still not common couple violence.

Common Couple Violence

Common couple violence occurs in response to ongoing conflict. Although the short-term objective may be for you to stop the other person from doing something, the violence is usually a result of frustration or anger. It is also random. It can be initiated either by you or by your partner. It doesn't occur with increasing frequency and is not planned or part of some larger plan.

To prevent future common couple violence, make a vow to yourself, without insisting he does the same, that you will no longer get physical with your partner, whether he provokes you or not. Become a role model for resolving conflict without the use of force. You should already be familiar with the signs when a blowup is imminent, so once you see the initial signs, back away from a physical confrontation. Develop a strategy for preventing future fights. Look for patterns to the violence in your relationship. Is it when you are both drinking or when you are high? If so, substances may be aggravating the problem, which, in turn, creates or increases the chances for violence. In general, avoid bringing up relationship issues during these times.

Employ anger management techniques. For example, try to identify your triggers. Write them down so that you can avoid them by increasing your awareness. When you are triggered, count to ten or take a deep breath before reacting. If things escalate while you are arguing with your partner, tell him you are going to take a break. Be sure to let him know you will come back once you have cooled down. Try using relaxation tapes or meditation; if you are more relaxed, you will have more patience when your fuse is short.

To put an end to common couple violence, outside intervention is usually required. This is because violence is a way to communicate what you have not been able to put into words. Learning how to communicate your thoughts and feelings more effectively can channel the anger and frustration into productive arguments. Because you're unable to do that, a therapist can help you change your pattern of relating. You may have to see your own individual therapist to discover why your feelings develop with such force that you need to come to physical blows. Odds are that you are funneling hurt into rage, and you need to examine the issues that go beyond your current relationship to see what's really going on.

Domestic Violence

Domestic violence is a systematic attempt by a perpetrator to control his partner (the victim) by acting abusively. Abuse includes using threats, intimidation, bullying, physical violence, and emotional and psychological violence. Physical violence includes hitting, biting, pushing, shoving, and kicking. Intimidation includes threats of violence to restrict where you go, whom you associate with, what you say, and what you do.

Sometimes it's hard to detect domestic violence when it's happening because it starts out subtly. One subtle form of abuse is emotional blackmail. For example, a perpetrator will threaten his partner with retaliation, such as withholding affection, when the victim does something he doesn't like. The Silent Treatment is not in and of itself domestic violence. If, however, the perpetrator knows that his partner freaks out when he gives him the Silent Treatment and uses it as a way to control him, it's approaching abuse. He learns his victim's vulnerabilities and exploits them, so the threats can be particularly painful.

Other subtle ways a perpetrator controls his partner is by repeatedly telling him how disappointed he is and telling his partner he isn't intelligent or good looking. Years later, the victim believes the perpetrator when he tells him that no one else would want him. Less subtle forms of control, yet still hard to detect as such, include raging, name-calling, criticizing, and belittling. An abusive partner becomes more threatening and violent over time. When simply telling his partner to shut up doesn't work, for example, threatening with a slap or a punch is next.

Domestic violence is not about being angry or lacking control over one's actions. The perpetrator may *appear* angry when he becomes violent, and indeed he may be. But how does he handle his anger at work? What happened the last time he was stopped by a cop for speeding? If he had a problem with anger management, his violence would be spilling out at work, with friends and family, and just about everywhere else.

Domestic violence is deliberate and calculating; the sole purpose is trying to control the victim. A perpetrator tries to control his partner for several reasons. Behind the aggressive façade is a huge fear of being abandoned. The perpetrator controls his partner to be sure he doesn't leave. The perpetrator may be extremely jealous and uses control as a way to be sure his partner isn't having sex with other people. Alternatively, the perpetrator uses violence simply as a way to get what he wants. Ironically, a perpetrator sees himself as the victim, and he believes that if only his partner did everything he wanted, the relationship would be fine.

You might be thinking that you'd never let this happen to you. I must warn you: Every victim is a "me" who never thought it would happen. It's a mistake to think that victims of domestic violence come from violent homes because most do not (although most perpetrators do). Many perpetrators find partners who are emotionally stronger and more financially independent than themselves. Eventually, they start to wear their partners down through an insidious process in an effort to make the victims dependent on them, even though the victims were stronger initially.

Just how does it happen? If you have been dating someone for a while and he's treating you well, are you wondering whether he could be a perpetrator? Probably not. How could such a great guy be a perpetrator? If you're not sure, think about this Red Flag.

⚑ RED FLAG: *Is He a Perpetrator?*

Let's say you meet someone who sweeps you off your feet. He cares for you so much that within a few weeks, the first "I love you" has been spoken and he will talk about having you move in. He calls you two or three times a day and e-mails you every day at work with loving messages. He wants to know everything about you. He has you go on and on about yourself, and he isn't very forthcoming about himself because he is so focused on you. You are floating on a cloud.

A few months later, he asks you to not go to lunch with a certain coworker because he knows that the guy must be interested in you. He'll admit he's jealous, but says, "If you really loved me, you wouldn't have lunch with him." By then, it's several text-messages, a couple of e-mails, a phone call or two every day, and maybe dropping in occasionally at your workplace just to say hi. With the flowers coming into the office every few weeks, your coworkers tell you how lucky you are.

What they and you don't know yet is that he is setting the stage for controlling you. He wants to move quickly because he doesn't want you to figure out what's going on. Within six months or a year, the methods he used to lure you in—wanting to know everything about you, contacting you several times a day, and knowing whom you associate with—are the very methods he will use to control you.

Eventually, he starts putting you down. He may tell you that your cooking sucks or complain that he doesn't like the way you clean. You name it, and he will find a problem with it. You start to think you're not measuring up to his standards, and you may be concerned he will leave you. You feel stupid and inept, and it won't be long before he obliges you by telling you how dumb you are. Pretty soon, you do more things to please him and to keep him from criticizing you.

Because it is hard to put your finger on what is going on, you would naturally want to place the blame on yourself while your confidence erodes. Then, one day—maybe out of the blue—it happens. He pushes you. He will be apologetic and upset about his actions right away. If he was resting and you woke him up, he might tell you he pushed you as an automatic reflex. While you're at home, he might call you a nasty name; later, he might try to laugh it off with remarks such as "I was just kidding around" or "Can't you take a joke?"

Because you love your partner, and he has never done this before, of course you believe him. But a few weeks or months later, he does it again. This time, it's for a different reason, or maybe he tells you that you deserved it. You give him the benefit of the doubt and think that if you were better, he wouldn't do it again. The next day he is very sweet. He offers to take you out, apologizes profusely about what he did, and promises that he will never do it again because he doesn't want to hurt you. Repeated abuse is often followed by a period of remorse, known as the honeymoon. He may send you flowers or a nice gift.

The honeymoon lasts until the tension-building phase begins. During this phase, he becomes increasingly annoyed with you, and then confrontational. Again he tells you that you can't do anything right. You start walking on eggshells. As he gets angrier, you believe you are to blame for what's going on. You think that once you stop upsetting him, you can make the violence stop. But it doesn't, and violence is the conclusion of the tension-building phase. The violent phase is usually a much shorter time-span than the honeymoon or tension-building phases. Together, these three phases are known as the "cycle of violence," a phrase coined by the author Lenore Walker.

In addition to or instead of directing actual violence at you, he may try to intimidate you. He may harm your pet—or threaten to do so—break some of your things, or punch his fist through a wall. Even a certain look (the one that he adopted just before he hit you once before) can be used to intimidate you.

Sexual coercion is also a form of domestic violence. (I'm not talking about S&M sex, so don't confuse them. S&M involves two people entering into an act consensually, and the masochist is able to stop the action at any time). Some people believe that rape can't exist when you are in a relationship. If he forces you into having sex, it is rape. There are degrees of coercion, the less violent forms being the withholding of affection and outright threats of having sex with other men if you don't give him what he wants.

A perpetrator uses emotional and physical violence to make his partner feel ashamed, worthless, and confused *to control him.*

Why Victims Stay in Abusive Relationships

Reasons for staying in an abusive relationship are complex and difficult to understand. The shift from being treated like gold to being abused is a gradual process. It's under the radar because of the ability for the perpetrator to shift the blame and manipulate you.

One reason for staying in an abusive relationship is that the abuser has more power in the relationship. It may be difficult financially for you to live on your own, so the perpetrator creates situations to control you further. For example, he may move you into his place, and then a few months later tell you that you don't need to keep paying for a storage unit for your furniture, so you sell your belongings. Leaving just got much harder. He may tell you that you don't have to work any more—you're now a man of leisure. A year later, with no savings and no job, you're trapped.

You may stay because of his continual lies, which tend to be believable. A perpetrator might tell you that a friend or family member said something to him that was denigrating or mean. Examples include: "Your friend Bob came on to me. I don't think you should trust him" and "Your brother always interferes in our relationship, and every time you talk to him we get into a fight. If you care about me, you would stop talking to him."

The purpose of creating a wedge between you and your friends and family members is to isolate you. In the extreme, a perpetrator may convince you to move to another town or city, far away from your support system. As a result, you have no friends or family to turn to. These tactics increase the power difference, which facilitates

JEFFREY N. CHERNIN

further abuse, as well as more difficulty when it comes to leaving.

Another reason for staying is that the perpetrator has ways to make you feel responsible for the abuse. Examples include: "If you hadn't flirted with the waiter [even though you didn't], I wouldn't have hit you" and "Because I love you so much, I can't control myself." The problem is that with the repeated violence and threats of violence, it's easy to get confused and believe that what he's saying is true.

You might also stay because you feel threatened. For example, he may threaten to out you to coworkers or family members, an action that could lead to your being fired or ostracized. If you are deeply in the closet, the threat of being outed may be as threatening as his warnings that he will damage your property, kill your pet, injure you permanently, harm family members, or kill himself. He may also threaten to kill you if you leave. In fact, leaving is the most dangerous time.

Two other reasons for staying relate to the ways people learn to cope with overwhelming amounts of stress. One is called the Stockholm syndrome, the details of which are beyond the scope of this book. However, the result is a strong attachment to the perpetrator through magnifying the importance of acts of kindness while denying or minimizing the abuse. The other is posttraumatic stress disorder, and the symptoms include depression, dissociation, feelings of helplessness (and therefore increased dependence on the perpetrator), and brain dysfunction. One symptom is the blocking out of traumatic memories, a strategy that makes it possible for you to minimize the level of violence.

What to Do If Your Partner Is Abusive

If you have recently moved in together, look for signs of disrespect or dismissal. How is the power imbalance handled? If he makes more money than you, how does he deal with it? Do you talk about it, and is he sensitive to your feelings about making less money? A yes answer is a good sign. On the other hand, does he resist having you

180

make decisions? Does he refuse to let you pay for anything? When he doesn't get his way, do you get the Silent Treatment or a mind game? Does he yell at you, call you names, or belittle you? If so, you may be with a perpetrator.

If you want the relationship to work, your partner will have to be able to talk openly about the abuse, take responsibility for it, and give you not only a firm commitment that he will stop, but 100 percent compliance. A willingness to get into and stay in counseling means that he may get better. Couples counseling is not helpful if he's currently battering. (If he has stopped for a year or more, he *may* be a good candidate for couples counseling). The most effective form of treatment for him is a batterers' group, as opposed to an anger management group. Domestic violence is about control and not anger.

While he is in treatment, you may want to separate until he learns how to deal with his feelings of worthlessness, jealousy, and insecurity in a nonviolent manner. Find a therapist for yourself who has experience in dealing with abuse. If you are on a budget, try a low-cost agency.

Meanwhile, develop a safety plan for when the abuse happens again. Elements of a safety plan include what to do during three critical times: when a violent episode is imminent, when it's happening, and right after it occurs. Go to the Internet and search for "safety plans" and "domestic violence." If your partner is monitoring your Internet activities, use the Internet at a library, at work, or at a friend's house. Important parts of a safety plan include having hotline numbers and options for places to stay. As a last resort, you may have to go to a homeless shelter because so few cities have domestic violence shelters for male victims.

If he refuses to stop being violent, won't go for treatment, and isn't willing to take responsibility for the violence, your only option is to determine whether you can live in this kind of relationship. If you can't, develop a strategy to get out. Save money, borrow from family or friends, or stay with someone until you find a place. Strategize with family and friends to determine the safest and most practical way to leave.

If you're afraid of what he will do to you or your loved ones, including your children or pets, don't listen to others who insist you leave. They may not understand that you could be putting yourself or your loved ones in grave danger. You alone need to determine the proper timing of your departure.

Putting It Together

Several highly challenging barriers to intimacy, including substance abuse, mental illness, and relationship violence, are best addressed individually at first. Through diligent efforts by both partners, these issues can be successfully overcome. If you are willing to address these concerns but your partner is not, you may have no other choice but to reconsider your relationship. Either way, you grow and learn through your experiences.

In the last few chapters, we focused on several kinds of barriers to intimacy. All these circumstances impact your relationship by leaving it in need of repair. In the next chapter, we explore ways for you to restore intimacy that has been lost. These same tools can also be used for getting closer during the times when you and your partner are doing well.

CHAPTER 12

Communication Tools for Restoring and Enhancing Intimacy

TROUBLES WITH COMMUNICATING are at the center of most relationship challenges. When you and your partner learn to communicate more effectively, you increase the chances of resolving your issues successfully, ending frustrating dynamics, and getting closer. The topics we explored in the last several chapters—including socialization as a male, internalized homophobia, and other challenges to intimacy—can be addressed by using the tools offered in this chapter.

Restoring and Enhancing Intimacy

The most effective way of resolving relationship challenges to your mutual satisfaction is to accept responsibility for your part and to communicate openly. A vital aspect of communication is trying to understand your partner's point of view. As you explore options to resolve your differences, try to remove competition and one-upmanship by first acknowledging that you both have valid points of view. Open the lines of communication by taking your own and your partner's thoughts, feelings, and desires into account to the same degree as you take your own.

Whenever you're finding ways to maintain, enhance, or restore intimacy, you're also referring to receptive, open, and empathic ways to communicate. As psychotherapist Betty Berzon said in *The Intimacy Dance,* "Intimacy can be the greatest gift of a relationship—the person you know and can trust is there to comfort and protect you, no matter what. True intimacy means being with another without the self-protective strategies you may have employed in the past. It is the willingness to engage in dialogue and the skill to work through conflict that really makes for relationship success." There are many ways to enhance intimacy or to help get it back on track. Some ways to get closer to your partner include:

- *Become assertive*
- *Don't underestimate the impact of hellos and goodbyes*
- *Avoid second-guessing your partner's motives*
- *Use active listening*
- *Offer reassurance*

Become Assertive

You may find assertiveness to be a difficult form of communication. Sometimes assertiveness is confused with aggression, which is how we were socialized. Assertiveness is asking for what you want and being willing to take no for an answer. Aggression is not accepting it. Part of our socialization is thinking that we should get what we want simply by asking for it. Be prepared, however, for your partner to turn you down sometimes. Equally problematic is having been raised in a household where boundaries were violated and people told each other what to do. It can lead to believing that assertiveness should be avoided because it looks like confrontation, which turned into yelling or punishment.

That's why when something is bothering you, you can use a model called Empathy-Conflict-Action to be more assertive. An Empathy statement is a statement of understanding. You are letting your partner know why he would think a certain way or do something in a particular way. A Conflict statement means stating what the problem is for you or the situation you're hoping to address. Finally, an Action statement is what you're asking him to do. See diagram 12.1 for a summary of the model.

EMPATHY ⟶ **CONFLICT** ⟶ **ACTION**
Statement of   The problem   What do
understanding   you want?

FIGURE 12.1: EMPATHY-CONFLICT-ACTION MODEL

As an example of how you might use the model, consider public displays of affection, but this time let's say that you're uncomfortable in certain circumstances. You approach your partner with the following:

Empathy statement: "I really like holding hands and I appreciate how affectionate you are. I know you like to be spontaneous, and when we're in the gay part of town, I like when you touch me."

Conflict statement: "I'm not as out as you are, and I know this is my stuff. But I still get uncomfortable sometimes when we're in public. When we're not in the gay part of town, it doesn't feel natural to me."

Action statement: "I'd like you to ask me first when we're not in the gay area."

The Empathy statement acknowledges that you know he's affectionate and spontaneous, and you like both qualities. The Conflict statement comes in when you say you are still uncomfortable holding hands when you're not in the gay area. One drawback of this model is the use of the term "conflict." One way to see this is simply what you're uncomfortable or upset about. The Action statement is how you want him to address the issue, in this example to limit holding hands when the two of you are not in the gay area.

Use "I" Statements

Part of being assertive is to use "I" statements when you want to talk to your partner about something he's doing that upsets you. Focus on what he did, followed by the way you feel, so he can understand how his action affects you. When you use "I" statements, specify an action as opposed to a trait. For example, mentioning to your partner that he isn't picking up his clothes is more likely to lead to a productive discussion than accusing him of being lazy. Telling him he isn't picking up after himself is indisputable. So are your feelings about it, be they frustration, annoyance, or anger. When you concretely identify the action you're unhappy with, you open the door to a discussion.

Vs. "You" Statements

When you begin a statement with "You," especially when followed by "always" or "never," your partner is apt to become defensive. This opens the door to moving away from the subject at hand. Keep in mind that a statement such as "You never listen to me" isn't going to generate a productive discussion.

A sentence starting with "I think you …" is a "You" statement in disguise. For example, "I think you said that because you don't care about me" will most likely make your partner protest your statement. As an alternative, say something along the lines of "When you didn't call me, I was annoyed." This assertion is a statement of fact, and it describes how you feel because of what happened.

Stick to the Subject

The only way you and your partner can resolve a problem is to stay focused on working on it. As you think about this, here are two illustrations. Take 1 is an example of how not sticking to the subject leads to a stalemate and creates emotional distance. Take 2 is the same argument but revised to illustrate sticking to the subject. For both takes, let's say that you come home with a television you have just purchased. Your partner is angry because you previously agreed to make major purchases together. As soon as your partner sees you with the television, he says, "What the hell is that?" You reply, *"It's the TV I told you I was going to buy."* "I asked you to wait until I had thought about it some more. And besides, you can't tell me anything." *"I didn't tell you. I can't help it if you misunderstood."* "Don't you dare turn this around on me. You always ignore me and do what you want."

Take 1:

"I don't ignore you. You're the one who ignores me. I asked you if it's OK to buy the TV, and you nodded your head like you always do when you aren't paying attention to me. But it doesn't matter because you never listen to me." "I always listen to you, but sometimes you go on and on and have nothing to say." *"Are you saying I'm boring? That's really mean."* "If I'm so mean, why do you stay in this relationship?"

Take 1 would leave you both fuming. Now let's try Take 2. You realize where this could be heading, and so you catch yourself to avoid a potential blowout as you work your way back to the original subject.

Take 2:

After he mentions that you ignore him, you say: *"It bothers me to think I ignore you, but right now we're talking about my buying a TV and your anger about it."* "It's not just about the television. The problem is that you never listen to me." *"We can get into that subject later. Right now, we're talking about the TV. Maybe we miscommunicated. I thought you said it's okay for me to buy it. But because we can't agree on what we decided, I'll take it back."* "Fine. Take it back. Wait, I don't know. It would be a hassle. Let me think about it. Maybe it is the one I wanted." *"I'm sorry. For the next big purchase we can go together, or I can remind you what I think you agreed to before leaving for the store. I can still take it back."*

Notice in Take 2 that you redirected your partner twice. The first time was when your partner complained that you ignore him and the second time was when he accused you of not listening. By redirecting your partner back to the subject, you didn't allow the argument to escalate. Your partner may still be angry about thinking he wasn't consulted, but you avoid becoming emotionally distant, and you're laying the groundwork for an agreement for future purchases.

Let Your Partner Know When You Just Want Him to Listen

Not all communication requires a response, especially when a situation doesn't have a solution. Recall that the way we were socialized is that if there's a problem, we need to fix it. However, if you are more into sharing your feelings than your partner is, ask him to listen and not respond. If your partner is results-oriented (wants to find solutions), and you have a situation where you just want to vent, it's okay to tell him ahead of time that you're not into "solution mode." If the situation involves him, he may feel the need to respond. So if it's about an ongoing situation between you, ask him to sleep on it before responding.

Likewise, if you're more results-oriented, that's great in certain areas of your life, and even sometimes in your relationship, but it can inhibit intimacy. Offer advice or suggestions only when your partner asks. Otherwise, try to become a better "container" for your partner and his feelings. It may mean getting in touch with some uncomfortable feelings, especially helplessness. You may need to literally and figuratively sit on your hands as you listen. We look at several ways to be a better listener in the active listening section.

Don't Underestimate the Impact of Hellos and Goodbyes

Every time you meet, you set the tone for your time together. Sometimes you may need to negotiate your greetings, such as when each of you gets home from work. For example, let's say you're able to come home from work, change clothes, and settle in for the evening in five minutes. On the other hand, your partner needs time to unwind before changing gears. He needs twenty minutes to read his mail, change clothes, and listen to his phone messages. If so, let him have some time, in spite of your being excited to see him or wanting to talk. In general, get to know and respect his coming-home needs.

If your partner has a lousy day at work and comes home in a bad mood, what happens when he arrives? When he's had a bad day and can't shake his mood, do you sometimes mistakenly think it's because of something you've done? If so, ask him to let you know that he's grumpy from his day when he walks in the door. That way, you can give him some extra space when he gets home and additional time for him to vent about his day. At the same time, you won't wonder what's wrong or assume he's upset with you.

Likewise, saying goodbye in a pleasant way sets the tone for your next greeting. If you leave without saying goodbye, you're indirectly communicating indifference. On the other hand, it's possible to develop an adult form of "separation anxiety." Being unaware of not wanting to separate, you become ornery, indifferent, or upset when it's time to part. When you're going to be away from your partner for an extended period, it's easier to be angry than to be sad. Right before parting, avoid starting an argument.

As another example, most people have different needs when waking up and going to bed. In the morning, some people hit the snooze button, but others spring out of bed. As a general rule, respect your partner's way of greeting the world. If he likes to "emerge," you can get up and start your day quietly while he rests.

When it comes to conflicting needs, look at how important the issue is for each of you. Let's say you prefer to stay up later than your partner, but your partner tells you it's really important to go to bed at the same time or else he can't fall asleep. You have your answer about how to negotiate bedtime because the one with the stronger rationale and feelings should be accommodated. If the issue is equally important to both of you, it requires more creative solutions. Continuing the example, let's say you stay up to watch television because it helps you fall asleep. You could both go to bed at the same time, and you could watch the news while he goes to sleep. If the noise bothers him, he can use earplugs to shut out the noise. What if the earplugs annoy him and he can't fall asleep with them in his ears? You could use headphones and press the mute button. If the light bothers him, ask him to use an eye mask.

Avoid Second-Guessing Your Partner's Motives

Second-guessing your partner's motives starts with making an assumption about why your partner does something and then stating it as fact. For instance, let's say he was going to be late for dinner and didn't inform you beforehand. Instead of sticking with what he did and then telling him how it affects you—inconvenience, annoyance, and irritation—you assume that he did it because he's uncaring and thoughtless.

Consider how you might be assuming the nature of your partner's motives. For example, saying "You didn't call me because you were trying to get back at me for last week when I was late" is assuming a spiteful motive. Other examples include "You did that because you're trying to hurt me" (a malicious motive); "You don't like my friends because you're not the center of attention" (a jealous motive); and "You only do it when you want to" (a selfish motive).

One reason to avoid second-guessing your partner's motives is that you are attacking his character. Additionally, you're making him the enemy instead of giving him the benefit of the doubt, such as being forgetful, miscommunicating, and, above all, not intentionally trying to hurt you. Conversely, if your partner second-guesses your motives, let him know that it hurts you, makes you feel angry, and causes you to feel badly about him, the relationship, and yourself.

Another reason to steer clear of second-guessing his motives is because you are possibly missing the issues that lie beneath your assumptions. In other words, deeper issues such as trust, responsibility, and honesty could be lurking below. If you have questions about these issues, bring them up directly instead of accusing him indirectly. By doing so, you are bringing the deeper issues to the surface. And it could help you answer an important question: "How much of this particular problem is due to me, my partner, and our dynamics?"

Moreover, when you make an assumption about why your partner does something, you may be unwittingly revealing more about yourself than about your partner. By assuming what motivates him, you may be projecting. Think about the times you have said to your partner, "You did this to me because of such-and-such." If you can't come up with an example, think about it the next time you make an assumption about why he does something. When you have projection, your assumption would actually be *your* motives and not necessarily his. It could also be that you're unconsciously mistaking him for an important person from your past.

The ideal situation is to assume that your partner is on the same team and has your best interests at heart. But when you must second-guess his motives, try to consider several possibilities instead of just one. Considering an array of possibilities is a way to ameliorate feelings that come up as a result of your first, somewhat automatic, thought about why your partner did something. Alternatively, have your question start with "Could it be . . . " or "Are you . . . "—such as in the example "Did you not call me back because you're mad at me?" Your partner may react more receptively than if you assume you're correct.

Use Active Listening

The phrase "you're not listening to me" should not be taken literally. It means that communication has become bogged down. Active listening tries to correct interrupting, discounting, and other ways of not listening to each other. For instance, when you're having a discussion with your partner and it turns into an argument, you are now thinking about what you're going to say in response to what he says. Because you're thinking, you can't understand what your partner is saying. The intensity of your feelings has an inverse relationship to your ability to listen. When you're really angry, you can't listen at all. The end result is that each of you is trying to be heard, which can lead to yelling, withdrawal, and emotional distance.

Active listening also helps you consider your timing. When you tend to have a strong emotional reaction, let some time pass. You will hear your partner better when you discuss an issue in a relaxed atmosphere, perhaps over coffee or a meal. When you have something to bring up, ask whether it's a good time to talk about it; don't just start in on what you want to say. But don't wait too long, either. By waiting too long, you and your partner have less accurate recall. You learn how long is too long by trial and error. As a general rule, wait no more than a few days.

Active listening is attempting to understand your partner by asking questions to solicit more information and to rephrase or summarize what your partner is saying. When you are actively listening, if what he is saying is unclear or incomplete, ask a question for clarification. The purpose of asking a question is not to interrogate him or to attack his position. Rather, seek out more information and be sure you understand what your partner intends to say. After you have listened and asked questions to clarify, respond to your partner's statement by summarizing out loud what you've heard. Wait until he has completed his thought before responding.

Avoid interpreting or putting a spin on what you think he meant. Simply review what you heard. When you finish paraphrasing, see whether he corrects you before you continue. If he corrects you, try again. Summarizing out loud what your partner says is a temporary way to do what will eventually feel natural, and then you can do it silently. Once he is satisfied that you have heard him, respond to what he's saying with your thoughts and feelings. You are not trying to defend yourself when you use this tool. What you are attempting to do is to open up communication by doing your best to understand your partner.

For additional assistance, you could temporarily use a talking stick, which is a Native American tradition used during negotiations (communications expert Palden Jenkins refers to it as a "listening stick," which is an equally good name, maybe better). The person holding the talking stick is the one who gets to talk. The other person's job is to listen, nod, and limit responses to "I see," "Mmm-hmm," and "Yes" (known as "encouragers"). The other person gets his turn when the talking stick is handed over. Each person's turn is limited to a couple of minutes. This technique is helpful because it acts as a reminder to listen instead of formulating what you're going to say next, and it prevents the tendency to interrupt. This makes the atmosphere for communication more relaxed and therefore more conducive to productive dialogue.

You can use anything to symbolize a talking stick, such as a pen or the remote. Or you can make one. Couples have told me that using the talking stick is awkward at first and even feels silly. I ask them whether they laugh when it feels ridiculous and they generally say yes. However, anything that interrupts your pattern enhances communication, and laughing together helps build intimacy as well. So if the talking stick causes a change in the way you relate to each other, the process itself can create a shift.

Eventually, whether you use the stick or not, talking this new way can begin to feel natural, and once it feels comfortable, you no longer need to summarize your partner's comments out loud. Remember that a major goal of active listening is to increase empathy toward each other. You can empathize only when you seek to understand him. As you contemplate employing this new approach, consider how Alex and Mark have made progress on changing the relationship dynamic they had already begun to resolve in chapter 8.

CASE STUDY: *Alex and Mark*
After their last episode, during which Mark had some time to think about how his withdrawing and running out of the house was hurting their relationship, he approaches Alex to talk about it. Alex is pleased with

himself because he waited and he's equally pleased that Mark wants to talk. Mark asks Alex to talk first about what's bothering him, as Mark actively listens.

Alex: "When you run into the bedroom and leave the house, it brings up this panic in me." Mark (to seek more information): "Do you know where the panic comes from?" Alex: "Yes. My parents used to fight a lot, and when things got bad, my dad would storm out of the house. I'd be watching and it'd freak me out." Mark (summarizing): "So you would panic when your dad left." Alex (slightly correcting him): "Not when he left, but before, because I was scared to death that he would leave and never come back, which is what happens between you and me." Mark (summarizing): "So you start panicking before I leave, when our fights escalate." Alex: "Exactly, and that's why I get so agitated and raise my voice. I'm scared you're going to leave." Mark: "So you're trying to get me to stay by raising your voice. Our fights bring up horrible memories for you." Alex: "Yes, and I'd really appreciate it if you wouldn't leave."

Mark feels heard and understood, and now it is his turn to listen actively to Alex. Mark: "You raise your voice to try to get me to stay, but it drives me away. You are getting exactly the opposite response to what you want." Alex (summarizing): "I'm shooting myself in the foot." Mark: "That's right. I can't handle being yelled at. It makes me want to run. I need for you to talk to me calmly and rationally." Alex (summarizing): "So if I talk to you in a normal voice, you won't run." Mark: "Yes."

Alex and Mark both feel heard and understood. They are moving past their old relationship dynamic into new ways of relating to each other. They are learning to have productive dialogue and are feeling closer.

Active listening isn't just a technique. Your partner wants exactly what you want: To be heard and understood. Truly listening is a way to validate each other, to empathize, to show consideration, and to be respectful.

Offer Reassurance

During periods of fighting and distance, reassure your partner that you aren't going anywhere and you still care for him. It's natural for him to feel insecure when your relationship is going through rough times. Your partner may get anxious about the issue you're talking about because he is worried that you will leave him. Once he is reassured, he can calm down. If you are the one who gets anxious, it's okay to ask your partner for reassurance during your arguments, including reassuring words and hugs.

Apologize

When conflict arises, you and your partner will at times hurt each other. Partly as a result of our socialization as males, you may think that the person who is right doesn't have to apologize. However, when he is upset, an apology helps reduce hurt feelings regardless of who is right. An apology is complete only when you commit to yourself not to do it again.

Try not to qualify your apology. Don't say, for example, "I'm sorry because your feelings were hurt." Rather, say this: "I'm sorry for hurting you." Often, apologies are qualified (or not offered) because pride gets in the way. If you avoid apologizing to your partner, try it sometime just to see what kind of response you get and to see how you feel. It's humbling, and more than likely, when you acknowledge your part, your partner will acknowledge his role and will apologize to you. On the other hand, what if you're the one who always apologizes first and would like an apology from your partner? It may be awkward to ask, though you could say: "Y'know, I'm usually the one to apologize, but I'd like for you to occasionally apologize first."

Don't fool yourself into thinking that just because you apologize, all should be forgiven immediately. If you mistakenly believe that you think he should forget because you've apologized, perhaps you're using apologies as a way to persuade him to stop being angry with you. However, your partner may need some time to come around after the apology, and you should try to tolerate his anger.

Putting It Together

No matter which challenges you encounter, learning to communicate openly and creating a safe place for your partner by fostering open communication leads to better chances for resolution and for growing closer. Becoming assertive, using "I" statements, avoiding second-guessing his motives, and using active listening all contribute to solutions to ongoing conflict. However, certain tools and techniques go beyond communication and help with feelings of closeness. In the final chapter, I discuss techniques for reaching the ultimate goal of genuine intimacy.

CHAPTER 13

Achieving Genuine Intimacy

GENUINE INTIMACY IS achieved when you and your partner know each other on a meaningful level, but this can come about only when you have enjoyed many good times and survived several rough or transitional periods. You cannot see all of each other's traits, moods, and behaviors until you have been together for several years. Staying together once you accept each other, complete with faults and foibles, is the essence of genuine intimacy.

Ways to Achieve Genuine Intimacy

Here are some ways to progress toward genuine intimacy:

- *Look at the real reasons for conflict*
- *Be creative when resolving your differences*
- *Balance vulnerability and protection*
- *Separate thoughts from feelings*
- *Develop social interest*
- *Establish rituals*
- *Create a safe harbor*
- *Symbolize your commitment*

Look at the Real Reasons for Conflict

After a fight, how many times have you been unable to remember what you were fighting about? In addition to issues associated with relationship dynamics (discussed in chapters 7 and 8), the themes often represent larger issues. In the Take 1/Take 2 examples in the previous chapter, issues besides purchasing a television are coming up, and they need to be dealt with separately. During disagreements, you should try to stick to the subject, but it's important to see the signs that point to bigger issues that need to be addressed.

One way to determine whether larger issues are affecting you is when your conflicts have a theme. If it's confusing to figure out which disagreements have a theme, think about the arguments you have in which you could script out what you and your partner would say. You also generally know the outcome, which includes feeling hurt, angry, and distant. Here are a few themes to consider.

Obtaining Reassurance

When you want reassurance that your partner still cares about you but can't directly ask for it, fighting can indirectly do just that. While you and your partner argue, you are communicating that you each care enough to fight. However, there's a cost to intimacy because ongoing disagreements add to righteous feelings (digging your heels in) and emotional distance. Also, recall that it's sometimes hard to be vulnerable, especially when you have difficulty trusting others. If fighting and distance are ways that you're trying to gain reassurance, consider taking the risk of being more direct.

Trying to Get Your Partner to Meet All of Your Needs

Sometimes, a person goes into relationships thinking that his partner is supposed to meet his needs for friendship, companionship, support, and romance. As you know from your own disillusionment, your partner isn't the person you thought he was, and he cannot be the person who can give you everything you want. Trouble begins when you want him to be something he isn't. If you rely on him too much, he will ultimately frustrate your efforts by virtue of being human.

Testing Limits

This theme emerges when you or your partner has ambivalent feelings about intimacy. Assuming it's your partner who tests, he will let you in to a certain point, and then he will push you away. Part of the reason he is pushing you away is to see whether you'll go away. When you don't, you pass the test. Unfortunately, testing creates threats to intimacy because of its push-pull nature. Other underlying reasons for conflict include control and domination, lack of trust, fear of being abandoned, the need for space (or being threatened by a need for space), and insecurity.

Misinterpreting Your Feelings

Sometimes, you might confuse primitive emotions with feeling angry and irritable toward your partner. Remember when we considered how babies react when they are hungry, teething, or wet? They scream their heads off. Look at the timing of when you get irritable with your partner. Do you pick fights around dinnertime or bedtime? It could be because you are allowing sensations of hunger, fatigue, or even boredom to turn into anger directed at your partner.

Anger can also result from being depressed. Because we are socialized to hide our feelings, men are more likely than women to have what's called an "angry depression." It includes being irritable and developing a short fuse. You may be able to hide your symptoms for a while, but depression will bleed into your relationship. If you think you're depressed, let your partner know, and then take action to help yourself through it.

Displacing Your Anger

Whether it's from stress at work or some other source, you may be directing anger toward your partner even though your negative feelings have nothing to do with him. It's similar to when a child is mistreated by his parents and peers: He responds by yelling at the dog. In other words, you don't think you are able to direct your anger at the source. For example, your boss yells at you, so you take it out on your partner. You may not be aware you're doing this. When you become aware, realize it's unfair to your partner, and he is going to start taking protective actions. This makes corrective action important for intimacy and for the relationship itself.

Be Creative When Resolving Your Differences

When it comes to resolving your differences, the ends are no more important than the means. The means should include respect, warmth, and empathy. You may need some trial-and-error before you hit on the combination that works. For example, in the heat of an argument over something, immediately acknowledge your contribution. It could stop the disagreement in its tracks. As another example, when you're upset with your partner, instead of arguing, let him know you're going to cool off until your anger subsides. Then approach your partner and offer him a hug or a smile before continuing. Talk about your feelings as a result of what happened. Not only will your partner appreciate your efforts, but he will also see you as a role model for his own behavior.

Consider "His Stuff" to be "Our Stuff"

When your partner has a problem, part of being creative is to realize that it's now your problem in the sense that both of you will be dealing with it. Thinking that something is "his stuff" discounts your partner and his feelings. Instead, think about ways to take your partner's issues into account. When your partner has a sensitive area, your job is to go around the button and not push it. Let's say that your partner has issues with authority, and when you tell him to do something (rather than ask him), he gets mad. A "that's his stuff" approach would translate into continuing to tell him what to do and thinking he should just get over it. An "our stuff" approach means exploring why it's important to him that you ask and then adjusting the way you approach him.

Find the Humor

Part of being creative is trying to find humor in situations you find exasperating or frustrating. For example, let's say the remote control is important to the point where you argue over it. When you end up fighting for the remote, what can you say or do to make it funny? Turn it into a game or laugh at yourself for being immature about it. Stay in touch with your playful side for your own well-being, as well as for maintaining intimacy. It's essential to intimacy that you are playful with your partner. Laughter and lightheartedness should be part of your relationship.

If your partner has a quirky past or a character trait, it's okay to tease him lightly about it. Likewise, you should be self-effacing enough to accept gentle teasing from him. For example, laughing together about his being klutzy can generate positive feelings toward each other. You can have a running joke about certain experiences. If he is sensitive about something, however, you may want to consider the possibility that you're pushing his buttons rather than teasing.

Balance Vulnerability and Protection

A relationship is the one place in your life where you can find friendship, sexual fulfillment, and emotional closeness on the one hand while you expose yourself to being vulnerable, hurt, and rejected on the other. The balance between seeking closeness and protecting your vulnerability is a theoretical ideal. No one can always be open to being hurt and be self-protected at the same time. Let's take an extreme example: Your partner is deciding between staying in the relationship and leaving. You may have the mistaken notion that you must pull back to protect yourself. You might think that if he's reevaluating the relationship, then so should you. It's a mistake to do this as well as to demand a full and unwavering commitment from your partner all the time. There will be times when he questions the relationship, and these feelings are natural.

If your partner starts to seriously consider whether he wants to be in the relationship, and he informs you of this, then he is enrolling you in the process of making his decision. If he enrolls you, he is giving you the opportunity to explore what's not working. Instead of a knee-jerk reaction of pulling back or getting defensive, you have the option of stating your intention of making the relationship work. Nonetheless, everyone has emotional limits to handling the uncertainty, and you have the right to let him know you will not be able to handle this challenging feeling indefinitely. You can also enroll him when you know that you're getting close to being unable to handle the uncertainty much longer.

Separate Thoughts from Feelings

Communication can get bogged down when you confuse a thought with a feeling. For example, your partner asks, "How did you feel about what happened?" You reply, "I feel that you shouldn't have hurt me like that" or "I feel you were wrong." These statements are examples of thoughts (specifically, they are opinions). Examples of feelings are anger, hurt, and confusion. He can argue with your opinions, but he cannot disagree with how you feel. You can get your point across when you talk about how something he did caused you to feel. If he attempts to dismiss your feelings, stand firm.

When you cut yourself off from your feelings or won't express them directly, you can harm intimacy because feelings demand to be expressed. They will make themselves known, one way or another. For example, you may deny feeling hurt when your partner does something, but the feeling will be expressed by complaining to friends, pouting, going quiet, or funneling it into anger. The energy may also go into relationship escapes, such as alcohol and drugs, work, or sex outside the relationship. When you express your feelings directly, he can address what's going on, which creates closeness. If you're having trouble getting to know your feelings, obtain a "feeling chart" (also sometimes known as a "feeling wheel"), a tool that describes dozens of emotions.

Use your feelings as information about your relationship and yourself. Are you continually feeling hurt in your relationship? Does this mean that you have become a victim or martyr? On the other hand, do you need to protect yourself from someone who is intentionally hurtful? Although you are entitled to your feelings and can use them as a way of gathering information, feeling something doesn't require acting on it. For example, if you want to yell at your partner because you're feeling particularly angry, you increase intimacy by calmly telling your partner about the level of your anger and your desire to yell.

Use a "When you do such-and such, I feel . . . " approach to expressing your feelings. To illustrate, imagine that your partner has agreed to discuss social plans with you prior to making them. He's been pretty good about it overall, but in the last few weeks he has been slipping. You can say something like this: "When you agreed to talk to me first before making plans for both of us, I was relieved. You are aware of my feelings, and though you haven't been 100 percent, it's been good enough for me, which is why I haven't said anything. But I'm getting frustrated because you're going back on your word. You've agreed to go to dinner twice without consulting me. So please remember to talk to me first."

Don't Justify Your Feelings

Part of separating thoughts from feelings is to recognize that your feelings don't need to be justified. Expressing your feelings only when you *should* feel that way is not helpful in resolving conflicts. Start with the premise that you *do* feel this way. It doesn't matter whether your feelings are justified, acceptable, or right. They are part of you and they follow some kind of logic, even when they don't appear to. When you feel okay with the feelings that come up for you, you are more likely to share them with your partner. As you do, you are increasing communication, and therefore, closeness.

Likewise, your partner doesn't have right or wrong feelings. They are simply feelings, and any attempts to tell him he shouldn't feel that way could be a cover-up for emotions that are uncomfortable for you, of which guilt may be one. Try to avoid reacting to your partner by defending yourself when he talks to you about feelings of hurt or anger that have been caused by something you did. Most likely, you both have valid points and logical conclusions about who is right and who is wrong. However, belaboring those points won't get you anywhere; instead, look into why he feels this way and how you contributed to it.

Develop Social Interest

Alfred Adler, the psychology pioneer whom I first mentioned in chapter 7, used interest in other people's interests as a way to measure the health of relationships. You're able to determine your relationship health by the amount of social interest you have in your partner's well-being, needs, and desires. The more you develop an interest in your partner's interests, the more connected you feel. To maintain a strong connection with your partner, develop an interest in the important areas of work, friends, and family.

But not all social interest involves these major areas. For an illustration of how to take an interest in your partner's interests, consider the following situation. Let's say that your partner loves opera, but you don't really care for it. Over the years, you learned why he likes certain operas more than others and that Puccini is his favorite composer.

Because you have made the effort to know about your partner's interests and have a basic understanding of them, you have developed social interest by trying to appreciate the art form and why your partner is such an avid fan. When your partner starts to bubble over with enthusiasm about a new recording or an upcoming opera, you are able to keep up with him, and he is sharing an important part of his life with you.

The Platinum Rule

This discussion leads us to the platinum rule. It's great to do nice things for each other. Unfortunately, many of us use the golden rule, which is doing to him what you would like done to you. The platinum rule takes the golden rule to the next step: Do things for him and give him gifts you know he would enjoy, even if it's not something you would like. Consider how you might use the platinum rule as you read about Roberto and David's situation.

CASE STUDY: *Roberto and David*

After a few years of being together, Roberto started to wonder—even though David acts appreciatively when Roberto sends him flowers and cards—whether David likes receiving them. One day, Roberto asks David what he thinks of his cards and flowers. David takes a deep breath and replies, "I really appreciate the sentiment, but I am not as crazy about getting card and flowers as you are. I feel loved when you give me a foot rub or back rub, or just hold me." Though Roberto imagined this would be David's answer, he feels stung.

David knows he has hurt Roberto, so the next day he sends Roberto a dozen roses at work with a message that says, "From now on, you're the one to receive cards and flowers." Both David and Roberto arrive home from work that night feeling good about the turn of events. The next night, Roberto offers David a foot rub. With these two pieces of new information, each of them is able to give what the other partner truly wants

The Even-Steven Error

The flip side of the platinum rule is the even-Steven error, which occurs when you and your partner feel that you need to abide by the same guidelines. For example, let's say you read the paper together each morning. Your partner doesn't want you to discuss articles with him before he's had a chance to read them. Let's also assume that you don't mind. In this way, it's okay to treat each other differently. The following exercise helps you determine which decisions are based on the even-Steven error.

★ EXERCISE: HONE IN ON THE EVEN-STEVEN ERROR

Take a moment to think about the different ways that you and your partner want to be treated and things that don't really matter to one of you but they upset or bother the other. For example, your partner hates being shushed, but you don't really mind.

Once you have thought of a few, take out a piece of paper and list the items, along with possible solutions. One solution to the previous example would be to ask your partner how he wants to be treated when you want to ask him to be quiet. After you have finished your list, place it somewhere easily accessible to you. Occasionally look at the list as a reminder.

Another way to incorporate social interest in your relationship is to consider your motives for wanting to change your partner and ways you attempt it. When you have a problem with your partner, you can lodge complaints against him, try to belittle or shame him into changing, or attempt to overpower him. You can take a social interest approach, however, by voicing your concerns and encouraging him to grow as a person. At the same time, back away from pressuring him to change. Ironically, this approach creates an environment where your partner will feel safe to learn and grow.

For example, let's say that your partner has been having a hard time with his weight. If you approach him in a socially uninterested way, you will tell your partner that he's getting fat, puff your cheeks out when he reaches for the snacks, scold him when he overeats, and tell him to "get off your ass and exercise." If you are an even more socially uninterested person, you will threaten that if he doesn't lose some weight, you're going to get your sexual needs met with someone else.

As a person with social interest, on the other hand, you will feel concerned about your partner's weight gain. You will move your own needs and judgments aside and perhaps sit your partner down and ask him what's going on. Just as Roberto's talk with David illustrated, it's better not to hide your feelings about the situation; but you can approach your partner in a way that will show consideration and respect for his feelings. Approaching this issue with caring and warmth may help your partner realize that there could be more to his eating habits than meets the eye, and he may be more inclined to take action knowing that he has your support.

To continue to be socially interested, you could ask your partner whether there's anything you're doing that is contributing to his stress level. If you're receptive, you may hear that the stress he's having that leads him to overeat is associated with the relationship—and therefore with you. You could also ask your partner whether there's anything you can do in relation to the underlying issue and the overeating itself. For example, regarding an underlying issue, you could ask, "When I snap at you, does that contribute to your anxiety, which leads to eating?" When it comes to overeating, you could ask, "Should we keep certain foods out of the house?" "Should we share meals when we go out to eat?" Finally, instead of telling your partner to "get off his ass" and exercise, you could wake up on a Saturday morning and say, "Let's take a walk" (with the dog, if you have one). Or "Come with me to my yoga class (or to the gym)."

Establish Rituals

Intimacy is enhanced when you have frequent shared experiences that are enjoyable for both of you. Your lives may be busy, but you still need to share quality time to remain close. One way is to develop rituals. When I refer to rituals, I'm not talking about anything elaborate. Some rituals develop naturally as you spend time together. Going on hikes, eating breakfast together, and reading the Sunday paper are three rituals. Others can be more deliberate and planned. As you think about creating rituals, here's a way David and Roberto developed one.

CASE STUDY: *Roberto and David*

For their fourth anniversary, David painted a picture and gave it to Roberto. As Roberto looks at it, he notices small lettering on the perimeter of the painting. He looks at it more closely and realizes that David has written out everything special that the two of them have done together during the year. Because Roberto is so delighted, David decides to do this every year, using different media. One year, he paints on large coffee cups. Another year, he does calligraphy.

You may not have the artistic predisposition David has, but it's possible, without any talent, to create a book for your partner that lists special events throughout the year. Buy a blank journal and write events in the book, or type them on the computer and paste them onto the pages. You can further ritualize it by taking turns writing the entries or saving some space on the pages for your partner's reactions.

Think about what kind of rituals you and your partner could incorporate into your relationship. Keep in mind it can be simple, and that you ritualize something by lifting it out of the ordinary. For example, you already eat dinner together several times a week. Ritualize it by lighting a candle once a week. If you regularly eat in front of the television, occasionally eat at the dinner table. Or let's say you both take baths. Take them together sometimes, or wash your partner's hair or soap him down while he is taking his.

Another way to ritualize your relationship is to continue dating your partner. Remember when you were dating? Remember the feelings of anticipation you had and how you enjoyed being together? When you are already in a relationship, dates are for renewal, rejuvenation, and romance. Call your partner at work during the week and ask him out to a movie or dinner. On the evening of the date, bring him some flowers or a bottle of wine. While you are on the date, speak to each other the way you did when you first met. Be romantic at the end of the date, whether it leads to sex or not.

Create a Safe Harbor

Naturally you want to be in a relationship where you experience security, stability, closeness, and emotional and physical safety. When you have a lot of stress and pressure in other areas of your life, you have an even greater need for your relationship to be a safe harbor. What do you need to do to create an oasis for your partner? Strive toward some ideals to create one. When you act this way most of the time, you will be creating the foundation for closeness and lasting intimacy. These qualities include being able to accept your partner for who he is, being trustworthy and honest, and caring about him as you try to understand him and his feelings. Throughout your life together, you will be showing him a high level of respect as you balance your needs with his.

If you take a look at the first chapter, these are the same ingredients as being ready for intimacy. The difference between considering these qualities now as opposed to the way we looked at them in chapter 1 is to consider them in the context of your relationship and its dynamics. For instance, as you feel more secure in the relationship, your coping strategies (defenses) decrease. Your overall trust level increases, and you are able to avoid disagreements that you now know stem from outside sources such as discrimination and being socialized to be aggressive and competitive. You also know to handle issues such as harmful relationship dynamics, drifting apart, and significant life transitions.

When you're honest with yourself, you can be honest with him and have the courage to accept the consequences for your honesty. As you respect yourself, your respect for him and generosity for his faults increase. You're able to consider his needs on the same par as yours, and he can express his feelings with the security that he will be respected. As you see his point of view as being as valid as yours, you consider yourselves to be equals.

With these elements in place, your relationship is a safe harbor for your partner. You consider his vulnerabilities as special places to be avoided. When you steer clear of them, as your dynamics shift and you are no longer activating your partner's earlier wounds, the relationship becomes a source of healing and growth. As you treat each other respectfully, you both have the opportunity to grow, to become more intimate, and to find the type of relationship you've been looking for, in which you feel connected, safe, protected, and loved.

Symbolize Your Commitment

Society has made it harder for gay male couples to settle down for the long-term. The impediments I have described throughout the book give rise to the idea that, in many ways, a commitment to our partners takes more courage, more work, and more trust than for heterosexual couples.

The word "commitment" can be loaded because for heterosexual couples it is tantamount to monogamy. For many gay male couples who prefer to be non-monogamous, the sense of commitment can be just as strong. A major difference I have seen is that gay male couples tend to be more honest with each other and willing to forgive when infidelity strikes (whether it's straying from 100 percent monogamy or a betrayal of the rules). In fact, we have a lot to offer heterosexual couples in terms of what commitment is really about. So when I refer to commitment, I mean that a person is creating an intention to be with his partner for the long-term. For some people, this means for life. Others have a relationship that lasts ten, fifteen, or twenty years—but their sense of commitment and loyalty to each other is just as powerful if the relationship were to transition to a friendship.

Many gay men want to declare their love for one another publicly. Some do it by making a legally binding commitment in states or countries where it is legal for gay couples to marry or enter into a domestic partnership. Some combine the legal contract with a commitment ceremony or wedding, inviting friends and family to celebrate. Others choose not to enter into a legal commitment, but they have a public ceremony.

You can alternatively signify your commitment in other ways. For instance, you can create a ritual just for the two of you, such as exchanging rings or getting piercings or tattoos. How you symbolize your commitment is going to be up to you and your partner.

Because we have focused on getting closer, how you celebrate your love for each other can be left to the many good resources for planning rituals, weddings, and commitment ceremonies. As with any other issue I have raised in this book, the way you negotiate how to symbolize your commitment is as important as the event itself. Getting closer is related to how you treat each other on a daily basis before, during, and after.

To let you know what has happened with the couples and their relationships:

CASE STUDY: *Jason and Gregory*

Jason and Gregory were married by a Unitarian-Universalist minister. They invited several of their friends and families. Jason has been sober for several years, and he is a sponsor in the program. Although much of his energy is toward his sobriety and away from Gregory, it helps them stay together. They started talking about adopting a child, and they are in the process of finding an agency.

CASE STUDY: *Roberto and David*

Roberto and David found rings they liked and they bought them for each other for their tenth anniversary. They continue to live apart and are comfortable with their arrangement. They still have issues from time to time that arise from spirituality differences and disagreements about sex outside the relationship, but they approach these issues with respect and concern for one another and themselves. That, along with a sense of humor, gets them through their rough patches.

CASE STUDY: *Alex and Mark*

Alex and Mark are still trying to work things out. They are committed to the relationship but they aren't out of the woods yet. They know it will be a while before they can see eye-to-eye on many issues. Because of their dedication to making their relationship work, they appreciate each other's efforts. They foresee a future. Together.

Putting It Together

You and your partner create genuine intimacy when you learn to accept each other, communicate openly without fear of judgment or criticism, work through conflicts, and overcome threats to the relationship. In so doing, your relationship becomes a place where you assist each other with personal growth, contribute to each other's quality of life, and value a friend and companion. Above all, you create a genuine connection, share your life with someone, and at last have the intimacy you desire.

Appendix: Resources

Organizations

COUPLES NATIONAL NETWORK
Umbrella group for social and informational events for couples.
www.couples-national.org

FREEDOM TO MARRY
A gay and non-gay partnership working to win marriage equality
nationwide. www.freedomtomarry.org

HIV AND RELATIONSHIPS
www.hivandrelationships.com

LAMDA LEGAL DEFENSE & EDUCATION FUND
Legal advocacy, education, and litigation to secure dignity and
respect for same-sex relationships. www.lamdalegal.org

PARTNER'S TASK FORCE FOR GAY & LESBIAN COUPLES
National resources for same-sex couples. www.buddybuddy.com

STOP ABUSE FOR EVERYONE (SAFE)
Information and resources for sexual minorities who face domestic
violence. www.safe4all.org

ALCOHOLISM AND RECOVERY
www.gayalcoholics.com

NATIONAL ASSOCIATION OF LGBT COMMUNITY CENTERS
Supports and enhances (LGBT) community centers, with links to
more than 100 centers. www.lgbtcenters.org

PARENTS AND FRIENDS OF LESBIANS AND GAY MEN
(PFLAG)
Educational and support organization promoting the health and
well-being of LGBT individuals and their families. www.pflag.org

Books

Berzon, Betty. 2004. *Permanent Partners: Building Gay and Lesbian
Relationships That Last.* Revised edition. Plume. New York.

Burda, Joan. 2004. *Estate Planning for Same-Sex Couples.* American
Bar Association. Washington, D.C.

Curry, Hayden, et al. 2005. *A Legal Guide for Lesbian and Gay
Couples.* NOLO. Berkeley, CA.

Hazel, Dann. 1999. *Moving On: The Gay Man's Guide for Coping
When a Relationship Ends.* Kensington. New York.

Isensee, Rik. 2005. *Love Between Men: Enhancing Intimacy and
Resolving Conflicts in Gay Relationships.* Prentice Hall. Englewood
Cliffs, NJ.

Lustig, Harold. 1999. *4 Steps to Financial Security for Lesbian and
Gay Couples.* Ballantine Books. New York.

APPENDIX

Savage, Dan. 2005. *The Commitment: Love, Sex, Marriage, and My Family.* Dutton. New York.

Silverstein, Charles, and Felice Picano. 2004. *The New Joy of Gay Sex.* Collins. New York.

INDEX

A

abandonment, fear of, 96, 124
abusive relationships. *see* relationship violence
acceptance, in intimacy, 2
Action statement, in Empathy-Conflict-Action model, 184–185
active listening, as communication tool, 191–194
addiction, 167–172
    coming to terms with substance abuse, 167–168
    crystal meth, 168–169
    dealing with a partner who is addicted, 169–172
    in relationship dynamics, 104–105
Adler, Alfred, 105
adoption, 18
affection, public displays of, 138
aggressiveness
    affect on intimacy, 140–141
    assertiveness vs., 139, 184
    passive-aggressiveness, 141
Alanon, 170
Alex and Mark case study
    active listening, 193–194
    independence, regaining, 81
    moving in together, 57–58
    not keeping a lid on conflicts, 89–90
    outcome of their relationship, 211
    overview of, xiii
    power struggles, 71–72
    pursuer-withdrawer dynamic, 119–120
    relationship dynamics, 110–112
    struggle around friendships, 88–89
alone time, 18
anger. *see also* relationship violence
    aggressiveness and, 140–141
    apology to reduce partner's, 195–196
    competitiveness and, 146–147
    displacing, 199–200
    hiding vulnerability with, 146
    not indulging reactivity, 96
    in relationship dynamics, 116
anger management, 173, 176
angry depression
    dealing with a partner who has, 173
    looking at real reasons for conflict, 199
anxiety
    fear of abandonment and, 96
    threats causing, 86
apologies, reducing hurt feelings, 195–196
arguments. *see also* conflicts; power struggles
    cashing in on past infractions, 76
    hot-button words, 73
    needing the last word, 76–77
    not asking friends or family to referee, 94–95
    round-and-round, 73–74
    theoretical, 77
assertiveness, 184–190
    boys socialized for, 139
    Empathy-Conflict-Action model for, 184–185
    as form of communication, 184
    "I" statements vs. "You" statements, 186
    letting your partner know when you want him to listen, 188
    sticking to subject, 186–188
assets, protecting, 152–153
assumptions
    avoiding in active listening, 192
    second-guessing partner's motives, 190–191
attack-defend patterns, in communication, 77–78
attractiveness, concerns regarding, 25
availability, for personal feedback, 19
awkwardness, in dating, 28

B

bait-and-switch, 74–75
bank accounts, 152–153
bars, meeting places, 30–31
bathhouses, meeting places, 30–31
bedtime, negotiating, 189–190
bickering, as power struggle, 71
Birdcage (La Cage aux Folles), The, 13
book resources, 214
bookstores, meeting places, 30–31
boundaries
    counteracting family's homophobia with, 134
    not violating trust by talking to others about
    your relational problems, 94
    respecting partner's, 97–98
    revealing personal information and, 39
boyfriends. *see also* partners
    bringing up ex-boyfriends sabotages early
    intimacy, 45
    making plans to meet your boyfriend's family,
    48
boys, socialization of, 139
breakups, stopping the revolving door, 52–56
bushes, meeting places, 30–31
business aspect, of relationships, 6

C

carefree. *see* caretaker-carefree dynamic
caregivers, 106–107
caretaker role, substance abuse and, 168
caretaker-carefree dynamic
    changing dynamics of, 128–129
    lack of cooperation in, 162
    overview of, 115–116
caring, and respect in building intimacy, 9
cashing in, on past infractions, 76
chameleon effect, 75
cheating, destructiveness of, 155–159
childhood, relationship dynamics rooted in,
    108–110, 121–122
children
    adoption or conception, 18
    coping strategies, 108
    parenting, 106–107
cleanliness, values and preferences, 17–18
clinginess, 45
closeness and distance
    being able to tolerate fluctuations in, 21
    coping with periods of emotional distance, 82
    ebb and flow in relational process, 1
    in relationship dynamics, 100
codependency, in substance abuse, 168
coming out
    anonymous sexual encounters and, 23
    patience with partner's process, 138
    readiness for relationship and, 12–13
    supporting each other in, 136–137
commitment
    readiness for relationship and, 23
    symbolizing, 210–211
common couple violence, 173–175
communication
    assertiveness as form of, 184
    attack-defend patterns in, 77–78
    common couple violence and, 173–174
    patterns, 104
    in relationship dynamics, 101
    role in changing relationship dynamics, 118
    saying what you intend, 97
communication tools, 183–196
    active listening, 191–194
    assertiveness, 184–188
    avoid second-guessing partner's motives,
    190–191
    hellos and goodbyes, 188–190
    overview of, 183–184
    reassurance, 195–196
competition, male socialization and, 146–147
complaints, not complaining to friends and family
    about partner, 94
conception, values and preferences, 18
condoms, requiring in open relationships, 158
confidences, trust and, 7
Conflict statement, in Empathy-Conflict-Action
    model, 184–185
conflicts. *see also* arguments; power struggles
    danger of not keeping a lid on, 89–90
    hot-button words, 73
    picking a fight to gain reassurance, 82
    productive, 75–76
    real reasons for, 197–200
    vicious cycle in, 101
connection/connectedness, in intimacy, 2
control. *see also* power struggles
    aggression vs., 140
    domestic violence purposed to, 175–176
    identifying perpetrators, 176–179
    letting go of controlling your partner, 85–87

why victims stay in abusive relationships, 179–180
conversation
  starting a conversation, 29–30
  topics for first dates, 36–37
cooperation
  deepening intimacy and, 91–93
  as flexibility, 148
  lack of, 161–162
  as remedy for competitiveness, 147
coping strategies
  addicted partner, 170
  automaticity of, 119
  development in children, 108
  homophobia, xi–xii
  mentally ill partner, 172–173
  substance abuse, 167–168
  why victims stay in abusive relationships, 180
counseling
  breaking cycle of short-term relationships, 55–56
  closing escape hatches, 166
  common couple violence and, 173–174
  lack of cooperation and, 162
  what to do if partner is abusive, 181
courage, to change relationship dynamics, 123
criticizer. see pleaser-criticizer dynamic
crystal meth, 168–171
cycle of violence, 178

D

dating available men. see meeting/dating available men
dating partner, 208
dating services, Internet, 31–32
David. see Roberto and David case study
decision making, business aspect of relationships, 61
denial, substance abuse and, 167–168
dependability, vulnerability and trust and, 8
dependence. see also independence
  ability to reveal dependence or neediness, 141–142
  not being dependent on a partner for happiness, 21
depression, angry, 173, 199
desire, vs. fear in early intimacy, 52
desperation, fear of intimacy and, 54–55

differences in relationships
  exercise examining, 68–69
  highlighting, 65–68
  positive orientation to, 90–91
  power and, 148
  relationship dynamics and, 102
  Roberto and David case study, 69–70
  spirituality, 69
discrimination
  challenges to intimacy, 136–137
  internalized homophobia as, 137–138
disillusionment, end of honeymoon period, 63–64
distance and closeness. see closeness and distance
domestic violence. see also relationship violence
  defined, 173
  overview of, 175–176
  in relationship dynamics, 104–105
drifting apart
  closing escape hatches, 164–166
  overview of, 163
  relationship escapes, 163–164
driver's seat, in early intimacy, 44–45
drugs, in relationship dynamics, 104–105. see also substance abuse

E

early intimacy, 42–56
  challenges during, 50–52
  the driver's seat, 44–45
  five ways to sabotage, 45–46
  honeymoon period, 49–50
  Jason and Gregory case study, 42–43
  opening door to intimacy, 43–44
  overview of, 42
  stopping the revolving door, 52–56
  transitioning to a relationship, 47–49
e-mail
  exchanging after first date, 40
  relationships, 32–33
embarrassment, sensitive areas resulting in, 4. see also shame
emotional blackmail abuse, 175–176
emotional wounds, 6
emotions. see also feelings
  active listening and, 192
  common couple violence and, 173–174
  coping with periods of emotional distance, 82
  hiding/revealing, 55
  infancy and, 105

misinterpreting, 199
not justifying, 203–204
in relationship dynamics, 100
separating thoughts from, 202–204
sexually transmitted diseases and, 159–161
sharing vs. holding back, 143–145
empathy
increasing through active listening, 193–194
resolving differences creatively, 200–201
Empathy-Conflict-Action model, 184–185
enabling, substance abuse and, 168, 170
even-Steven error, 205–206
ex-boyfriends, sabotaging early intimacy by
bringing up, 45
exclusivity, transitioning from dating to
relationship, 48
expectations, changing as means of deepening
intimacy, 85

F

family. *see also* support system
differences between partners based on, 67
exercise in discovering family dynamics,
122–123
holidays and special occasions and, 135–136
influence on readiness for relationship, 11–12
meeting your boyfriend's family, 48
not complaining to family about partner, 94
not using to referee arguments with partner,
94–95
role models in relationship dynamics, 105
socialization of boys, 139
supportive and nonsupportive, 131–135
unsympathetic or critical attitudes of, 4
fears
of abandonment, 96, 124
based on previous relationships, 11
vs. desire in early intimacy, 52
domestic violence and, 173, 175–176
exercise assessing fear of intimacy, 52–56
feelings. *see also* emotions
hiding/revealing, 55
in relationship dynamics, 104
sharing vs. holding back, 143–145
fetishes, 26
finances
business aspect of relationships, 61–62
handling financially unstable partner, 152–153
moving in together, 59

overview of financial problems, 150–152
values and preferences, 16
what to do if partner is abusive, 180–182
first date, 35–38
concerns/factors, 35–36
Jason and Gregory case study, 38–39
revealing personal information, 38
what to avoid, 37–38
what to talk about, 36–37
where to go, 36
flexibility, true intimacy and, 148
friends
mutual friend as basis for meeting available
men, 27–29
not complaining to friends about partner, 94
not using to referee arguments with partner,
94–95
process of making friends, 43
fulfillment, in relationship dynamics, 116–117
future plans, transitioning from dating to
relationship, 47

G

gay men. *see also* males, societal pressures
committed relationships and, 23
personal growth and, xii
relationship challenges of, xi
short-term relationships and, 50–51
standards of appearance and, 25
genuine intimacy. *see* intimacy, achieving genuine
"good boy", relationship dynamic, 111
goodbyes, negotiating, 189–190
greetings, negotiating, 188–190
growing apart
closing escape hatches, 164–166
overview of, 163
relationship escapes, 163–164
guilt
exercise for reducing feelings of shame and
guilt, 5–6
sensitive areas resulting in, 4–5
violating rules for outside sex and, 159

H

hellos, negotiating, 189
hepatitis, 22, 159–161
herpes, 22, 159–161

heterosexuals, comparing process of short-term relationships, 50–51

HIV
  challenges of, 159–161
  communicating concerns regarding, 43
  readiness for relationship and, 22

holidays, family issues, 135–136

homophobia
  counteracting your family's, 134
  discrimination and challenges to intimacy, 136–137
  gay men dealing with, xi
  internalized, 137–139

honesty. *see also* truthfulness
  being honest without being brutal, 8
  creating safe harbor, 209–210
  destructiveness of cheating on your partner, 155–159
  idealism and, 65
  resenting violations of, 141
  second-guessing partner's motives and, 190–191
  values and preferences, 15

honeymoon period
  in early intimacy, 49–50
  end coinciding with moving in together, 63

hot-button words, 73

household chores, business aspect of relationships, 61

humor, resolving differences with, 200–201

hurtful ("you are _____ ") comments, avoiding, 95

I

"I Dunno" trap, 74–75

"I" statements, assertiveness and, 186

idealism
  high or unrealistic expectations, 85
  real intimacy vs., 65

indecision, "I Dunno" trap, 74–75

independence
  boys socialized for, 139
  not being dependent on a partner for happiness, 21
  regaining, 80–81, 127
  revealing dependence or neediness, 141–142

Individual Psychology (Adler), 105

infatuation
  fading, 63

honeymoon period and, 49

inferiority, parents and caregivers role in, 106–107

insecurity/security
  need for control and, 86
  readiness for relationship and, 26
  in relationship dynamics, 104
  uncovering unresolved issues, 21

internalized homophobia, 137–139

Internet
  blurring lines of monogamy, 159
  dating services, 31–32
  researching safety plan for domestic violence, 181

intimacy
  aggressiveness and, 140–141
  caring and respect and, 9
  challenges to gay men, 3–4
  definition of, 1–2, 184
  differences not a threat to, 65–68, 70
  discrimination as stressor to, 136–137
  early in relationships. *see* early intimacy
  family impact on gay relationships, 131–135
  fear of, 52–56
  finding and maintaining a relationship, x
  flexibility and, 148
  internalized homophobia as barrier to, 137–138
  opening door to, 43–44
  self protection as obstacle to, 1
  sensitive areas, 4–6
  sharing personal information, 9
  vulnerability and trust and, 7–8

intimacy, achieving genuine, 197–212
  balancing vulnerability and protection, 201–202
  creating safe harbor, 208–210
  developing social interest, 204–207
  establishing rituals, 207–208
  looking at real reasons for conflict, 197–200
  resolving differences creatively, 200–201
  separating thoughts from feelings, 202–204
  symbolizing your commitment, 210–211

intimacy, deepening, 84–99
  assessing your need to control, 86–87
  avoiding hurtful ("you are __") comments, 95
  changing expectations, 85
  cooperating and sharing power, 91–93
  getting beyond right and wrong, 87–89
  getting to underlying issues, 98
  keeping a lid on conflicts, 89–90

letting go of controlling, 85–86
letting partner know what makes you feel good, 98–99
not asking friends or family to referee your arguments, 94–95
not complaining to friends and family about partner, 94
not giving partner the silent treatment, 95–96
not indulging reactivity, 96
not manipulating partner, 93–94
overview of, 84
pleasing your partner, 98
positive orientation to differences, 90–91
respecting partner's boundaries, 97–98
saying what you intend, 97
intimacy, restoring/enhancing, 183–196
active listening, 191–194
avoid second-guessing partner's motives, 190–191
becoming assertive, 184–188
impact of hellos and goodbyes, 188–190
offering reassurance, 195–196
overview of, 183–184
intimacy, social issues affecting, 131–149
discrimination, 136–137
holidays and special occasions, 135–136
internalized homophobia, 137–139
societal pressures about males. see males, societal pressures
supportive and nonsupportive families, 131–135
intimacy, threats/challenges to, 150–182
drifting apart, 163–165
financially irresponsible partners, 150–153
lack of cooperation, 161–162
life transitions, 153–154
mental illness, 172–173
negotiating sexual limits, 155–159
relationship violence. see relationship violence
sexually transmitted disease, 159–161
substance abuse and addictions, 167–172
Intimacy Dance, The (Berzon), 184
intimidation, domestic violence and, 175–176, 178
isolation, internalized homophobia and, 138
issues. see problems/issues

J

Jason and Gregory case study
avoiding power struggles, 78–79
compromise in working out differences, 87–88
cooperation and sharing power, 91–93
early intimacy, 42–43
first date, 38–39
moving in together, 58–59
outcome of their relationship, 211
overview of, xiii, 2–3
second date, 40–41
sharing personal information, 2
substance abuse, 169
jealously, struggle around friendships, 88–89
joint accounts, handling financially unstable partner, 152–153

L

the last word, 76–77
lease, adding partner to, 60
legal issues, committed relationships and, 23
letting go
accepting differences, 67–68
of controlling your partner, 85–87
life transitions, challenges over time, 153–154
listening
active, 191–194
asking partner to listen and not respond, 188
listening stick, 193
loneliness, being able to tolerate fluctuations in closeness and distance, 21
long-distance relationships, 154

M

males, societal pressures, 139–148
aggression, 140–141
competition, 146–147
emotions, 143–145
fixing problems, 143–145
overview of, 139–140
questioning what it means to be a man, 148
strength and power, 141–142
tenderness and vulnerability, 145–146
valuing what we do, not what we are, 146–147
manipulation, not manipulating partner, 93–94
marriage, 23, 210–211
masturbation
limiting outside sex to mutual, 158
meeting sexual needs through, 146

meeting/dating available men
- bars, bathhouses, bookstores, and bushes, 30–31
- breakups and, 52–53
- first date, 35–38
- Internet, 31–33
- Jason and Gregory case study, 38–41
- mutual friend as basis for, 27–29
- political, religious, and social organizations for, 33–34
- the "prospect" of dating, 34–35
- public places for, 29–30
- second date, 39–40
- transitioning from dating to relationship, 47–49
- ways to meet available men, 27

mental illness, coping with in partner, 172–173

monogamy
- gay men and, 23
- Internet blurring lines of, 159
- negotiating sexual limits, 155–159
- sex and, 79–80
- symbolizing your commitment and, 210–211
- values and preferences, 16

morals, in value system, 13

moving in together
- Alex and Mark case study, 57–58
- deciding not to move in, 63
- to an existing place, 57–62
- Jason and Gregory case study, 58–59
- to a new place, 62–63
- transitioning from dating to relationship, 48–49

N

Nardi, Peter, 43
need, ability to reveal, 141–142. *see also* dependence
no-call-back rule, in open relationships, 158
nonjudgmental quality, caring and respect and, 9
notes, uses/abuses of in relationships, 71

O

one-down position, defined, 148
open relationships, rules for, 157–159
organization resources, 213–214

P

parenting, 106–107
parties, meeting/dating available men and, 29
partners
- abusive, 180–182
- avoid second-guessing motives of, 190–191
- communicating what makes you feel good, 98–99
- communicating when you want him to listen, 188
- dating, 208
- dealing with addiction of, 169–172
- destructiveness of cheating on, 155–159
- differences between based on family background, 67
- domestic violence and, 175–176
- encouraging growth of, 206–207
- financially irresponsible of, 150–153
- letting go of controlling, 85–86
- mentally ill, 172–173
- not complaining to friends and family about, 94
- not depending on for happiness, 21
- not expecting that your partner knows what is bothering you, 72
- not giving the silent treatment, 95–96
- not manipulating, 93–94
- not using family and friends to referee arguments with, 94–95
- patience coming our process of, 138
- pleasing, 98
- reassuring, 195–196
- resenting violations of trust, 141
- respecting boundaries, 97–98
- splitting rent/lease with, 60
- STD contracted by, 160

passive-aggressiveness, 141
patience, for partner's coming our process, 138
pedestal, falling off, 64–65
perfectionism, 114
perpetrators
- controlling partner in domestic violence, 175–176
- identifying potential, 176–179

personal ads, dating and, 32
personal growth
- factors in, xii
- gay men and, xii
- uncovering unresolved issues, 21
- working through issues, 19

personal information
  approaches to revealing, 38–39
  disclosing in process of developing intimacy, 43
  as litmus test, 44
  revealing on first date, 38
  sharing in building intimacy, 2–4
personal issues. *see* problems/issues
pickiness, fear of intimacy and, 55–56
platinum rule, 204–205
pleaser-criticizer dynamic
  changing dynamics of, 127–128
  overview of, 114–115
pleasing your partner, as means of deepening intimacy, 98
political organizations, for meeting/dating available men, 33–34
positive statements, 98–99
posttraumatic stress disorder, 180
power
  cooperation as means of dealing with power gap, 92
  giving up for sake of intimacy, 148
  identifying perpetrators of domestic violence, 176–179
  males socialized to be self-sufficient, 141–142
  recognizing differences in relationship, 148
  what to do if partner is abusive, 180–182
  why victims stay in abusive relationships, 179–180
power struggles. *see also* arguments; conflicts
  Alex and Mark case study, 71–72
  attack-defend patterns in communication, 77–78
  avoiding, 78–79
  bickering, 71
  cashing in on past infractions, 76
  chameleon effect, 75
  expecting that your partner knows what is bothering you, 72
  getting to underlying issues, 98
  hot-button words, 73
  "I Dunno" trap, 74–75
  making productive, 75–76
  navigating, 70
  needing the last word, 76–77
  notes, uses/abuses, 71
  picking your battles, 72–73
  the round-and-round, 73–74
  see-saw syndrome, 74
  theoretical arguments, 77

praise, 73
preferences, 15–19. *see also* values
privacy, withdrawers needing, 113
problems/issues
  attempts to resolve adding to relationship dynamics, 102
  families and holidays, 135–136
  financial, 150–152
  getting to underlying, 98
  legal issues in committed relationships, 23
  males socialized to fix, 143–145
  not emphasizing in early intimacy, 46
  not violating trust by talking to others about, 94
  social. *see* social issues
  solution mode, 143–145
  trust, 143
  uncovering unresolved, 21
professional goals, values and preferences, 16–17
projection, in relationship dynamics, 102–103
protection, balancing vulnerability and, 201–202
public places
  dating in public reduces discomfort of first dates, 36
  for meeting available men, 29–30
punishment, forms of, 73
pursuer-withdrawer dynamic
  Alex and Mark case study, 119–120
  changing dynamics of, 125–126
  overview of, 112–113

Q

qualities/traits, in relationship dynamics, 100
questions, in active listening, 192

R

rape, 178
Rational Recovery, 170
rationalization, of substance abuse, 167–168
reactivity
  changing the pattern of, 120
  finding ways to react differently, 118–119
  not indulging, 96
  responding vs. reacting, 120
reassurance
  being more direct about your need for, 198
  offering to partner, 195–196

recovery, dealing with a partner in, 170–171
rehab, dealing addicted partner, 170
rejection
    readiness for relationship and, 24–25
    vulnerability and trust and, 7
relationship dynamics, 100–117
    Alex and Mark case study, 110–112
    anger in, 116
    attempts to resolve problems add to, 102
    caretaker-carefree, 115–116
    emergence of, 103–104
    fulfillment in, 116–117
    harmful nature of, 100–101
    looking at real reasons for conflict, 197–200
    origins of, 104–108
    pleaser-criticizer, 114–115
    projection and, 102–103
    pursuer-withdrawer, 112–113
    rescuer-wounded bird, 113
    splitter, 116
    vicious cycle in, 101
    worldview and, 108–110
relationship dynamics, changing, 118–131
    caretaker-carefree, 128–129
    discovering family dynamics, 122–123
    finding ways to react differently, 118–119
    looking for the origin of the dynamic in
    childhood, 121–122
    pleaser-criticizer, 127–128
    pursuer-withdrawer, 119–120, 125–126
    realizing you are locked into a dynamic,
    120–121
    rescuer-wounded bird, 126–127
    responding vs. reacting, 120
    uncovering hidden goals, 123–124
relationship violence, 173–182
    common couple violence, 174–175
    cycle of, 178
    domestic violence, 175–176
    perpetrators, 176–178
    types of, 173
    what to do if partner is abusive, 180–182
    why victims stay in abusive relationships,
    179–180
relationships
    business aspect of, 61
    e-mail, 32–33
    long-distance, 154
    long-term, ix–x
    relationship vision, 18–19

    short-term, 50–51
    time to heal after s, 53
    transitioning from dating to, 47–49
relationships, building intimacy
    caring and respect, 9
    permanence, 8
    sensitive areas, 4–6
    sharing personal information, 2–4
    vulnerability and trust, 7–8
relationships, negotiating in a straight world,
    131–149
    discrimination, 136–137
    holidays and special occasions, 135–136
    internalized homophobia, 137–139
    societal pressures about males. *see* males,
    societal pressures
    supportive and nonsupportive families,
    131–135
relationships, new
    attack-defend patterns in communication,
    77–78
    bickering, 71
    cashing in on past infractions, 76
    challenges to, 63–64
    chameleon effect, 75
    conflicts, making productive vs. avoiding,
    75–76
    coping with periods of emotional distance, 82
    deciding not to move in, 63
    differences, 65–69
    falling off the pedestal, 64–65
    hot-button words, 73
    "I Dunno" trap, 74–75
    independence, regaining, 80–81
    moving into a new place, 62–63
    moving into an existing place, 57–62
    needing the last word, 76–77
    not expecting that your partner knows what is
    bothering you, 72
    notes, uses/abuses of, 71
    picking your battles, 72–73
    power struggles, 70–72, 78–79
    the round-and-round, 73–74
    see-saw syndrome, 74
    sex in, 79–80
    spirituality in, 69–70
    theoretical arguments, 77
relationships, readiness for, 11–26
    assessing values and preferences, 15–19
    attractiveness and, 25

coming out and, 12–13
committed relationships and, 23
evaluating, 20
factors impacting, 11–12
fetishes and, 26
HIV and STDs and, 22
not being dependent on a partner for happiness, 21
rejection and, 24–25
security/insecurity and, 26
trust and, 24
understanding how you come across to others, 19–20
value system and, 13–14
relationships, threats/challenges to, 150–182
drifting apart, 163–165
financially irresponsible partners, 150–153
lack of cooperation, 161–162
life transitions, 153–154
mental illness, 172–173
negotiating sexual limits, 155–159
relationship violence. *see* relationship violence
sexually transmitted disease, 159–161
substance abuse and addictions, 167–172
religious organizations, for meeting/dating available men, 33–34
rent, dividing with partner, 60
rescuer-wounded bird dynamic
changing dynamics of, 126–127
overview of, 113
wounded bird regaining independence, 127
resources
books, 214
organizations, 213–214
respect
boundaries and, 97–98
and caring in building intimacy, 9
cooperation fostering, 161–162
resolving differences creatively, 200–201
safe harbor created by, 209–210
supportive families providing, 132
values and preferences, 16
responsibility, accepting responsibility for relationship dynamics, 120–121
retaliation, projection and, 103
right and wrong, getting beyond, 87–89
rituals, developing, 207–208
Roberto and David case study
establishing rituals, 208
negotiating sex outside relationship, 155–156

outcome of their relationship, 211
overview of, xiii
platinum rule, 205
spiritual differences, 69–70
unsupportive family, 133–134
role models, 105
round-and-round, 73–74
routines, values and preferences and, 18
rules
for open relationships, 157–159
in value system, 13

S

S&M sex, 178
safe harbors, 208–210
safety plans, and domestic violence, 181
Save Ourselves, 170
saving money, values and preferences, 16
second dates
Jason and Gregory case study, 40–41
progressing to, 39–40
second-guessing, partner's motives, 190–191
secrets
coping with, 108
gay men dealing with homophobic beliefs, xi
shame and guilt and, 5
security. *see* insecurity/security
see-saw syndrome, 74
self-centeredness, 45
self-exploration, uncovering unresolved issues, 21
self-protection, 13
self-talk, 4
sensitive areas
building intimacy, 4–6
as litmus test, 44
opening door to intimacy, 43
trust and, 7–8
separation
development of in infancy, 106
separation anxiety, 189
sex
bars, bathhouses, bookstores, and bushes and, 30–31
closing escape hatches, 164–166
coercion as form of domestic violence, 178
communicating about sexual fetishes and preferences, 26
fear of vulnerability in regards to, 146

intimacy and, 43
negotiating limits in, 155–159
patterns in relationships, 79–80
relationship escape through outside, 165
rules for open relationships, 157–159
S&M, 178
sexually transmitted diseases, 159–161
when to talk about, 96
willingness to discuss, 22
shame
homophobic beliefs causing, x
internalized homophobia and, 137–138
sensitive areas resulting in, 4
sexual fetishes/preferences and, 26
shame and guilt, 5–6
shame spirals in children, 107
substance abuse and, 167–168
sharing feelings, 143–145
sharing personal information
in building intimacy, 2–4
exercise for reducing feelings of shame and
guilt, 5–6
sharing too much, too soon, 6
sharing power, 91–93
short-term relationships
breaking cycle of, 55–56
gay men and, x
overview of, 50–51
Silent Treatment
emotional blackmail abuse, 175
not giving partner the, 95–96
what to do if partner is abusive, 181
skills, for building intimacy, 42
social interests
developing, 204
even-Steven error, 205–206
platinum rule, 204–205
voicing concerns and encouraging growth of
partner, 206–207
social issues, 131–149
discrimination, 136–137
holidays and special occasions, 135–136
homophobic beliefs regarding long-term
relationships between gay men, 23
internalized homophobia, 137–139
societal pressures about males. *see* males,
societal pressures
supportive and nonsupportive families,
131–135
social organizations, for meeting/dating available

men, 33–34
sociability
pursuers and, 112
values and preferences, 17
solution mode, problems and, 143–145
special occasions, family issues, 135–136, 139–148
spirituality
differences in relationships, 69
exercise in assessing values and preferences, 17
Roberto and David case study, 69–70
splitter dynamic, 116
STDs (sexually transmitted diseases)
challenges of, 159–161
readiness for relationship and, 22
Stockholm syndrome, 180
strength, males socialized to be self-sufficient,
141–142
substance abuse, 167–172
causing common couple violence, 174
coming to terms with, 167–168
crystal meth, 168–169
dealing with a partner who is addicted,
169–172
family backgrounds impacting trust, 24
support system
changing relationship dynamics, 123
coping with mentally ill partner, 173
dealing with a partner who is addicted, 170
perpetrators convincing you to move away
from, 179–180
symbolizing your commitment, 210–211

T

talking stick, 192–193
tenderness, devaluing feelings of, 145–146
tension-building phase, in domestic violence, 178
testing limits, looking at real reasons for conflict,
198–199
theoretical arguments, 77
therapy. *see* counseling
thoughts, separating from feelings, 202–204
threats
anxiety caused by, 86
domestic violence and, 175–176
testing limits of relationship, 199
why victims stay in abusive relationships, 180
training relationships, xiv. *see also* short-term
relationships

traits/qualities, in relationship dynamics, 100

triggers, anger management and, 173

trust

    issues with, 143

    nonjudgmental quality and, 9

    partner contracting STD and, 160

    readiness for relationship and, 24

    safe harbor and, 209–210

    second-guessing partner's motives and, 190–191

    sharing personal information and, 3

    skepticism and doubt based on lack of, 11

    transitioning from dating to relationship, 47

    trusting experience more than words, 58

    values and preferences, 15

    vulnerability in building intimacy, 7–8

truthfulness. *see also* honesty

    coming out and, 13

    letting a date know when you are/are not interested, 39–40

    values and, 14

twelve-step program, for addiction, 170

U

ultimatums, dealing with addiction, 170–171

V

validation, from supportive families, 132

values

    affect of unsupportive families on, 132

    assessing, 15–19

    readiness for relationship and, 13–14

    what we do vs. what we are, 146–147

vicious cycle, relationship dynamics, 101

violence. *see* relationship violence

vulnerability

    ability to reveal dependence or neediness, 141–142

    balancing protection with, 201–202

    devaluing feelings of, 145–146

    reducing hurt feelings with apology, 195–196

    taking one-down position, 148

    transitioning from dating to relationship, 47

    and trust in building intimacy, 7–8

W

withdrawers. *see* pursuer-withdrawer dynamic

withdrawing, getting attention by, 121

worldview

    Alex and Mark, 125

    expressing, 108–110

    relationship patterns verifying, 124

wounded bird. *see* rescuer-wounded bird dynamic

Y

"You" statements

    assertiveness and, 186

    avoiding hurtful, 95